An Exploration of the Death Penalty

An Exploration of the
DEATH PENALTY

Austin Mardon, Catherine Mardon, Karen Therese Pangan, Irene
Falade, Benjamin A. Turner, Aleefa Devji, Alexa Gee

✣

GM
★
PRESS

Cover Design by Joshua Harnack
Typeset by Paige Prins

ISBN: 978-1-77369-816-8
eBook ISBN: 978-1-77369-817-5

Golden Meteorite Press
103 11919 82 St NW
Edmonton, AB T5B 2W3
www.goldenmeteoritepress.com

Contents

1

What is the Death Penalty?

by Benjamin A. Turner

The death penalty is a wide-ranging social phenomenon that has roots in the earliest human social groups. There are allowances for it in history related to criminal justice, social standards, religious rituals, and more. This book will focus on the use of death in various criminal justice systems and scenarios, the debate about its effectiveness and morality, the demographics of those most frequently affected, methods of execution, history of execution, current social views on the death penalty in the Canadian, American, and global context, reversal of death sentences, abolition of the death penalty in Europe, how the death penalty is portrayed in popular culture, and what issues are likely to impact the debate on the death penalty in the future. This chapter will provide a brief overview of many of the topics contained in subsequent chapters, and is intended to provide a primer for the book as a whole.

In Canada, the death penalty was abolished in 1976 (Rancourt, et al., 2020), and was last used to execute two convicted murderers in December 1962 (Rancourt, et al., 2020). It was first codified into the Canadian Criminal Code in 1892 with three categories: mandatory sentence for treason,the mandatory sentence for fatal or near-fatal piracy and murder, and optional for rape (Ryan, 1969). In 1954 the Criminal Code was amended with several important changes to the death penalty which included splitting treason into three categories: mandatory capital punishment, optional capital punishment, and non-capital (Ryan, 1969). Rape was dropped as a crime punishable by the death sentence, and the charges related to piracy and murder remained unchanged. It is a commonality in most jurisdictions that did or do have the death penalty for murder to be a capital crime. In the Canadian context, in the 40 years before the abolition of capital punishment the death penalty was only ever handed down for murder in the civilian context. Even then, death sentences for murder were relatively infrequent during that period as well (Ryan, 1969).

Public support for the death penalty was strong in Canada but the abolitionist movement gained traction following the Second World War, and even when abolition finally did take place initially it was the courts, not the elected government, that imposed the decision. Support for the death penalty led public opinion by a wide margin in 1976, making the court's decision, and later the government's, very unpopular (Ryan, 1969).

Proponents of the death penalty frequently offer two primary justifications: the perception that the death penalty is an effective deterrent for violent crime (Bengel, 2021), and that it is fitting retribution for the families of the victims of the perpetrator of a capital crime to lose their life (Baker, 1992). We will visit the former point first.

The deterrent theory states simply that if a criminal believes the state will execute them for their actions, it will help to keep criminals from committing serious crimes. That in a state where execution is not on the table, criminals will likely feel the government is soft on crime and that not only will they be less concerned with the consequences of their actions, but that perhaps the state will be more lenient in sentencing overall. This punitive approach was for a long time the primary justification for the death penalty in many jurisdictions and continues to enjoy broad support to this day in Canada and around the world. An internal report submitted to the government by the public service shortly before abolition indicated that there was statistical evidence to support the idea of a deterrent effect (Avio, 1979).

A time-series analysis conducted by Avio (1979) comparing the execution rate to the murder rate in Canada between 1920 and 1960 found no deterrent effect to the death penalty at all, however. Instead noting that while analysis is difficult because of the low number of executions in Canada, the murder rate was entirely unconnected to the number of executions conducted in that period. Abolitionists argue that death penalty supporters use anecdotal evidence to support their claims of the deterrent effect, while multiple statistical studies in various jurisdictions refute the presence of such a deterrent effect (Bengel, 2021). In other words, abolitionists commonly argue the death penalty cannot be justified by the deterrent effect because the deterrent effect is a myth.

The second common justification for the death penalty is less empirical, it is a question of ethics and values. Avio (1979) notes, "Complex (or simple, depending upon one's viewpoint) philosophic questions of justice perhaps play a more substantial role than deterrence in the formation of attitudes towards capital punishment" (pp. 670). These values relate to the idea that if a person commits murder, it is only fitting for the punishment to fit the crime and that they be killed. This viewpoint supports the idea that there is a role in the criminal justice system for retribution, not just rehabilitation (Levy, 2014). This view argues that true justice cannot simply focus on the reformation of criminals into productive members of society, but there must be some punitive element to give victims closure. This is a view that is supported by the heartbreaking account of Baker (1992), who was a former police officer. His son and friend were murdered in retaliation for an arrest Baker participated in, and he describes in detail the gut-wrenching reality of his feelings of guilt and anger of the deaths of two innocents who lost their lives simply because he was upholding the law as he had sworn to do. He felt that not only had he failed his son, but soon his anger at the perpetrator turned to the justice system as a whole for the drawn-out, convoluted process of handing down, upholding, and carrying out a death sentence. In his case it took 14 years for the matter to be settled, in the meantime, he felt he was unable to move on from his son's death because the drama of the legal case continued to unfold. In his view, the death penalty as a consequence of the murder of his son and the son's friend was justice, not revenge (Baker, 1992).

Baker had been a police officer for many years and had a good understanding of the foundations of the legal system. He had sworn to uphold a legal system that had the stated virtue that it is better to let 99 guilty parties go free than to punish one innocent (Baker, 1992). He argues that this approach places the rights of criminals above the rights of victims, particularly in his son's case. The idea is a potent one: that it is difficult for victims to find comfort in the lofty ideals of the legal system while having justice delayed or denied to them. It is important when considering this concept to appreciate that justice means something different to everyone, and there will inevitably be disagreements over what the justice system should look like because of this.

The abolitionist rebuttal to the idea that the death penalty is ethical because retribution is necessary for justice focuses on the idea of natural human rights (Bengel, 2021). The idea is that when a murderer is put in prison for life, they are giving up just as much as a person who is being executed, therefore practically speaking it is not necessary to execute the murderer for them to receive retribution. Moreover, it is a violation of human rights for the state to impose a death sentence, regardless of the crime, and such views are a relic from the past. Interestingly, demographic analysis in the United States of death penalty proponents demonstrates a link between political conservatism and pro-death penalty views (Haney, et al., 2022). This indicates that in the US, where the death penalty opinion is largely divided on party lines, it is part of a broader conversation about the character and future of the nation.

There is further practical reasoning that applies to the abolitionist argument that it is not necessary to kill someone to take away their life, and that is the element of uncertainty. Abolitionists argue that one major flaw with the death penalty is that we live in an imperfect world and that the systems people build are influenced and shaped by their individual biases both consciously and unconsciously. To that end, the death penalty is rejected by many abolitionists entirely because of the fallibility of human beings, and the finality of the punishment (Lynch, 2009). If a prisoner is given a life sentence for murder and new evidence comes to light exonerating them, the person can be released and allowed to resume their place in society. If the innocent person was executed, the sentence cannot be undone. While the imprisoned person can never get back the years they lost, they are still certainly in a better position than the person that cannot be brought back to life.

Haney, et al. (2022) note in their article that jury selection for capital cases in the US is particularly problematic. A higher standard is required of death penalty juries, including the willingness to utilize the death penalty. Those who favour the death penalty possess some concerning characteristics that skew these juries towards execution before the trial even begins. Surveys of adults in California, New Hampshire, and Florida indicate that those who are most likely to pass jury screening in death penalty cases are typically less racially diverse, and more likely to use aggravating factors such as socioeconomic factors to justify the use of the death penalty, and are more punitive generally (Haney, et al., 2022). These surveys support observations made by Rancout, et al. (2020) that say supporters of capital punishment in the US tend to be white, male, protestant, married, and politically conservative.

Returning to the Canadian context, there is very little data regarding current demographic statistics related to the death penalty, but what is known is that the subject is not polarized on the same political lines as in the US (Rancourt, et al., 2020). Public discourse in Canada has long been dead, more or less, regarding the death penalty; this despite a large minority of Canadians continue to support the death penalty. It would appear that even for those Canadians who support capital punishment, it is largely viewed as a settled matter. Data from 2015 indicates only 41% of Canadians support the death penalty, compared to 69% of Americans (Rancourt, et al., 2020). Even with such strong support for the death penalty among the public, there has only been one political party to make restoration of capital punishment part of their policy platforms: the Reform Party (1988-2000) (Rancourt, et al., 2020). One possible reason for this lack of interest among the political elite is that before the government codifying the ban on capital punishment, the Supreme Court put a moratorium on the practice first, deciding the practice to be unconstitutional. Therefore a government wishing to reinstate capital punishment would be required to invoke the notwithstanding clause of the constitution, which is politically very costly and with very little upside since very few in the body politic are calling for change. It would be a very expensive promise that almost nobody wants, but at the same time promising to invoke the notwithstanding clause is a political party saying out loud they wish to circumvent the Charter of Rights and Freedoms on that subject, not to mention the clause must be renewed every five years which keeps the controversy alive to the detriment of the governing party that exercises that option.

One element that has a great impact on support for the death penalty is culture. The sub-regions of East Asia and Southeast Asia generally have very high death penalty support, of the 16 nation-states in those regions 9 fall into the retentionist category of the death penalty. This out of 56 retentionist states globally (Holmes, 2020). Of the retentionist states in these regions, Japan is the most economically developed, and it is also one of the most active states that still impose the death penalty. Some death penalty supporters argue that Japan's low crime rate is a result of its frequent use of the death penalty (Bengel, 2021). One unique element of the death penalty in Japan is their use of the sentence not just for murder convictions, but also for corruption and organized crime (Holmes, 2020). Goel & Mazhar (2019) highlight that while there is no evidence for a deterrent effect on murder rates in death penalty jurisdictions, there is some evidence that white-collar crime is reduced by the death penalty.

Further research on this topic is required, but it makes sense that capital punishment would not be a deterrent to murder. Dr. Catherine Mardon notes that in all her years interviewing and representing convicted murderers in their death penalty appeals, she never met anyone sober and sane at the time of their crime (C. Mardon, personal communication, 19 May 2022). In her experience, the typical murderer does not have the capacity at the time of their crime to understand and weigh the consequences, so it does not matter whether the death penalty is in place for such an act. For white-collar crimes, on the other hand? Those who are in a position of authority and are corrupt, or those who participate in organized crime, their acts are calculated and sober events for which the perpetrator does conduct risk-reward analysis.

There are some caveats to the Goal & Mazhar (2019) research, however. They concede that the death penalty is less effective as a deterrent to corruption because people with authority that can be misused are also potentially in a position to interfere with the justice system in their jurisdiction, thus lowering the effectiveness of the penalties. The death penalty is only an effective deterrent to white-collar crime in jurisdictions where capital punishment is still used. States where death penalty laws are in place but the punishment is never used are categorized as abolitionist by practice, because even though the state technically retains the authority in their codified laws, the practical expressions of the justice system are different from the codified authority (Goel & Mazhar, 2019).

Canada was an abolitionist by practice state for nearly 20 years before the Supreme Court, followed by Parliament removed the practice. Other notable abolitionist by practice states include Russia and Brazil, despite both states enjoying 62% and 57% public support for the death penalty, respectively (Holmes, 2020).

The argument that Japan has a low crime rate because of the deterrent effect of the death penalty, therefore, may hold up if the discussion were related to organized crime and a lesser extent political corruption, but retentionists generally refer to the commission of violent crimes such as murder and for that there is no evidence that the death penalty is effective (C. Mardon, personal communication, 19 May 2022). The argument against deterrence is bolstered by the fact that, in abolitionist states such as Italy or Canada, no major shifts occurred in violent crime rates in the time since their death penalties were abolished (Bengel, 2021). There is an overlapping concept in the Japanese case that is evident in academic articles that may explain the low crime rate and high support for the death penalty: social norms. In Japan, there is a powerful influence of very conservative views about social norms, authority, and societal institutions (Bengel, 2021). These norms arguably contribute to a lower crime rate, but they also lend to the support for the death penalty. Across many jurisdictions demographic analysis indicates that race, religion, political conservatism, and gender are strong indicators of support for the death penalty; this is apparent in Japan, Brazil, and the United States (Boateng & Dzordzormenyoh, 2022, Haney, et al., 2022, Rancourt, et al., 2020).

In the context of Canada and the United States, an additional factor also appears to influence the debate: trust in government. In the United States, there is high mistrust of the government, and any attempt by elected officials to abolish the death penalty in their state is characterized by opponents as those officials being soft on crime, and untrustworthy with the safety and security of citizens (Rancourt, et al., 2020). It is a political strategy that has seen great success in recent years in that nation. In Canada, however, trust in government is relatively high and while there was support of over 70% in 1976, the year the penalty was abolished, it has seen a consistent downward trend to just 42% by 2015 (Rancourt, et al., 2020).

Room exists within the debate on the topic for nuance in perspective. Indeed nuance is already implied, after all, nobody argues the death penalty should be applied as the uniform punishment for all crimes. There are supporters of the death penalty who successfully argued at the US Supreme Court that a mentally handicapped person who commits murder is less culpable for the crime than an individual with a higher IQ score (Tepker, 2006, Wilson, 2016, C. Mardon, personal communication, 19 May 2022). So the execution of a person clinically demonstrated to have an IQ lower than 80 is legally barred in the United States, but the system is not without flaws. The result of the Ford v. Wainwright case established that an IQ test be used to establish the eligibility of a prisoner for the death penalty prior to sentencing (Wilson, 2016). The system can be circumvented, however, if testing conditions are not sterile. Before a prosecutor makes the application to a judge to try a death penalty case, the accused often has relatively incompetent legal representation. Typically a public defender that is just a few months out of law school, or not infrequently a lawyer that is older but suffering from addiction problems and without any independent practice of their own. In many cases, the prosecutor will request an IQ test be administered before their application for the death penalty is filed and a young public defender may not realize the purpose of an IQ test because they lack the experience of defending a client against the death penalty. It is not uncommon for the prosecution to administer the same test multiple times until the defendant passes the 80-point line, administering the same test over and over again skews the results upward; the effect can also happen at times when different tests are used because there are relatively few testing methods accepted by the courts and the defendant may learn from their previous experience (C. Mardon, personal communication, 19 May 2022). There are many people on death row in the United States who should not technically be eligible based on their IQ score, but for whom the prosecution manipulated results to pursue their desired outcome. For enthusiastic pro-death penalty district attorneys, they do not feel that the mentally handicapped are less culpable for the crime of murder than a more high-functioning individual.

There are those calling for the age of eligibility for the death penalty to be raised to 25 years old. In the case of Roper v. Simmons in 2005 the US Supreme Court ruled the execution of minors to be unconstitutional (Tepker, 2006). Those who are not yet the age of majority, like the mentally handicapped, are not considered legally as culpable for their crimes as other adults. Those arguing for the age of eligibility to be raised to 25 note the medical understanding of brain development and the fact that the human brain does not finish developing until the mid '20s, meaning that a 22-year-old is not mature enough to fully understand the implications and consequences of their actions (Stewart, 2021). Furthermore, it is argued that evolving standards of decency in public opinion and both national and international policies denounce the use of the death penalty for young offenders, although nothing binding has been passed so executions of offenders who were under the age of 25 continue to this day; a Supreme Court ruling or an act of Congress prohibiting the execution of these young offenders would also bring the United States in line with the United Nations Convention on the Rights of the Child, which has been ratified by a large number of nations but not yet the United States (Stewart, 2021). There is one more argument offered by the abolitionists on this matter, which is that young adults are more susceptible to antisocial peer pressure than their older counterparts (Stewart, 2021). In other words, a younger adult may be bullied into committing a crime that intentionally or unintentionally carries significant consequences, including execution.

As previously established in this chapter, in the United States the execution of the mentally handicapped and minors is prohibited by federal law. One group that has no protection is the mentally ill (Hanson, 2021). Someone can experience a mental illness that could temporarily leave them without the ability to understand the consequences of their actions, and the argument is that the same reasons the 8th amendment to the US Constitution protects the mentally handicapped and the underaged from execution should also apply to the mentally ill. It is possible in the current court system for a defendant to plead not guilty by reason of insanity, but this is a hazardous route to go because it does not afford additional protections for the defendant and it leaves the choice entirely in the hands of the jury. Jury selection, as discussed earlier in this chapter tends to filter for individuals that are more punitive and willing to use the death penalty, so for defendants hoping to use the insanity defence, there is still a significant risk that they will be executed for a crime they committed while too ill to make decisions.

In the state of Arizona, there are some lawyers are lobbying for structural changes to the way death penalty cases are handled. Their concern is not over whether the death penalty is ethical, these are not abolitionists, but they do highlight the inequities in the system that leads to significant injustice. In the US legal system, the person deciding whether a defendant faces the death penalty is not a judge or even a jury, the charge must be pressed by a District Attorney in the first place (C. Mardon, personal communication, 19 May 2022), which creates significant unequal application in how the death penalty is applied because District Attorneys are not held to the same standards as judges in their decision making (Cattani & McMurdie, 2021). In Arizona the proposal is to remove death penalty decisions from the county level and elevate them to the state level to ensure there is equal application of the law to all residents regardless of their location within the state; the change would add transparency and legitimacy to the process and ensure a more equal application of justice.

In one case discussed by Dr. Mardon (personal communication, 19 May 2022), she represented a defendant seeking to have his death penalty commuted so he could instead serve a life sentence without the possibility of parole. To highlight how unequal the death penalty is applied under the current system, she noted that despite there being two defendants in the original incident, both of whom participated equally in the murder, one received the death penalty and the other received a life sentence. The only difference in their respective court cases was the District Attorney that tried them. In a system where two men commit the same crime, at the same time, against the same victim, but one gets life and the other gets death, there is significant inequity taking place.

In another case, Dr. Mardon (personal communication, 19 May 2022) discussed her experience witnessing a lethal injection. She relayed how the family members of the victim were surprised after the murderer was pronounced dead, and how dissatisfied they all appeared. It was as if they felt their hurt would wash away the instant it was over, but there was no relief in it for them. She remarked that in her experience working on death penalty cases, there were only a small few who found any relief following the execution of the perpetrator and that because the process often takes 15 or 20 years to run its course most of the families become disillusioned with the legal system in a similar way to Baker (1992) (C. Mardon, personal communication, 19 May 2022).

For her part, Dr. Mardon was so shaken up by witnessing what she refers to as a botched execution, where the prisoner cried out in pain and struggled to breathe for an extensive period, that it ended her time working death row cases (C. Mardon, personal communication, 19 May 2022). The room was filled with family members of the victim who were, understandably, openly hostile to her. As the execution continued to draw on she was unsure of whether this was normal or not, until one of the guards lost consciousness from watching it and fell across several people in the viewing area. Then some of the witnesses became ill. It was a dramatic scene and not what one would consider a humane execution. What was almost as bad was that the charity group she worked for in representing death row inmates asked her to talk to the media afterwards, to use the event as a fundraising platform for the cause. In describing how she felt after that experience she described feeling like she was unclean, covered in an oily film that wouldn't wash off.

References

Avio, K. L. (1979). Capital Punishment in Canada: A Time-Series Analysis of the Deterrent Hypothesis. The Canadian Journal of Economics / Revue Canadienne d'Economique, 12(4), 647–676.

Baker, S. (1992). Justice not revenge: a crime victim's perspective on capital punishment. UCLA Law Review, 40(2), 339.

Bengel, E. (2021). Dying for the Rule of Law: Crime and Capital Punishment in Japan and Italy. Michigan State International Law Review, 29(1), 47–76.

Boateng, F. D., & Dzordzormenyoh, M. K. (2022). Capital Punishment in Brazil: Exploring Factors That Predict Public Support for the Death Penalty. Journal of Contemporary Criminal Justice, 38(1), 56–71. _

Britto, S., & Noga-Styron, K. E. (2015). The Belief That Guns Deter Crime and Support for Capital Punishment. Criminal Justice Studies: A Critical Journal of Crime, Law and Society, 28(3), 314–335.

Cattani, K. E., & McMurdie, P. J. (2021). Death Penalty 101: The Death Penalty Charging Decision in Arizona. Is There a Better Way? Arizona State Law Journal, 53(3), 793–803.

Goel, R. K., & Mazhar, U. (2019). Does capital punishment deter white collar crimes? World Economy, 42(6), 1873–1897.

Haney, C., Zurbriggen, E. L., & Weill, J. M. (2022). The continuing unfairness of death qualification: Changing death penalty attitudes and capital jury selection. Psychology, Public Policy, and Law, 28(1), 1–31.

HANSON, E. (2021). Cruel and Unusual: The Constitutional Requirement for Heightened Protections for Defendants with Severe Mental Illness in Capital Cases. Idaho Law Review, 57(2), 299–324.

Holmes, B. (2020). Secretive Symbolism? The Death Penalty, Executions, and Japan. *Criminal Law Forum*, 31(4), 579–601.

Levy, K. (2014). Why Retributivism Needs Consequentialism: The Rightful Place of Revenge in the Criminal Justice System. Rutgers Law Review, 66(3), 629–684.

Lynch, C. (2009). Indonesia's Use of Capital Punishment for Drug-Trafficking Crimes: Legal Obligations, Extralegal Factors, and the Bali Nine Case. Columbia Human Rights Law Review, 40(2), 523–594.

Kovarsky, L. (2022). The Trump Executions. Texas Law Review, 100(4), 621–681.

Rancourt, M., Ouellet, C., & Dufresne, Y. (2020). Is the death penalty debate really dead? Contrasting capital punishment support in Canada and the United States. Analyses of Social Issues and Public Policy (ASAP), 20(1), 536–562.

Ryan, S. (1969). Capital Punishment in Canada. The British Journal of Criminology, 9(1), 80–85.

STEWART, T. (2021). Capital Punishment of Young Adults in Light of Evolving Standards of Science and Decency: Why Ohio Should Raise the Minimum Age for Death Penalty Eligibility to Twenty-Five (25). Cleveland State Law Review, 70(1), 91–119.

Tepker, H. F. (2006). Tradition & the abolition of capital punishment for juvenile crime. Oklahoma Law Review, 59(4), 809.

Vernon, A. (2017). The Ethics of Appropriate Justice Approaches: Lessons from a Restorative Response to Institutional Abuse. Law in Context: A Socio-Legal Journal, 35(1), 139–158.

Welling, B., & Hipfner, L. A. (1976). Cruel and Unusual?: Capital Punishment in Canada. The University of Toronto Law Journal, 26(1), 55–83.

Wilson, R. J. (2016). The Death Penalty and Mental Illness in International Human Rights Law: Toward Abolition. Washington & Lee Law Review, 73(3), 1469–1499.

2

What is the History of the Death Penalty?

by Aleefa Devji

Going back through history, the death penalty, also referred to as capital punishment, was established as a disciplinary act for heinous crimes such as murder and the documentation of the death penalty can be traced back to 18th Century BC. During 18th Century B.C. the Babylonian King Hammurabi who reigned from 1792 B.C. to 1750 B.C. codified the death penalty within the Hammurabi code of laws. This code of laws was a collection of 282 rules, fines, and punishments that set the standard for business interactions and social conduct (Reggio, 1999). King Hammurabi's code was carved into a massive black stone pillar during this time, to figuratively set the code in stone.

The death penalty was not abolished with the end of the Babylonian era, but instead it continued to be prescribed throughout history. This punishment for crimes can be followed through to the establishment of other codes of law such as in the Hittite Code, the B.C.

Draconian Code of Athens, and then Roman Law of the Twelve Tablets and other Laws ("Early history of the death penalty," n.d.). The methods used for killing the individuals who were found guilty of the crimes that prescribed the death penalty were often cruel and included but were not limited to crucifixion, drowning at sea, being buried alive, being beaten to death, and being impaled. The Romans had an interesting method for condemning individuals guilty of parricides (murder of a parent or near relative), which was death by means of submersion in water after being put into a sack with a dog, rooster, a viper, and an ape (Reggio, 1999).

The Code of Hammurabi

The Code of Hammurabi, carved into a black stone pillar was from a single four-ton slab of diorite which is a durable stone but incredibly difficult to carve. The text carved into the stone is a scripture of legal precedents amongst texts celebrating Hammurabi's rule over Babylon. The legal precedents set in the Code of Hammurabi are known to be some of the earliest examples of retribution, also known as "an eye for an eye."

Written in this code there were 282 rules, all were written in an "if-then" format such that if a person commits a crime, then they would be punished in a specified way or have to pay a specified fine. It is noteworthy that the Code of Hammurabi also outlined different standards of justice based on the three classes of Babylonian society - the propertied class, freedmen, and slaves ("Hammurabi's code: An eye for an eye," n.d.). To better understand this concept of class based standards an example would be the cost for a doctor's visit which would be most expensive for a man of propertied class and least expensive for a slave. Likewise, the penalties for crime were based on the status or class of the victim such that if a doctor killed a man of propertied class in a malpractice suit they would have their hands cut off, but if the man was a slave the doctor would only be required to pay financial resistution.

King Hammurabi understood that there was a need for a universal set of laws to rule his diverse empire but was also keen on protecting widows, orphans and others from being harmed or exploited. Hammurabi stated that he wanted "to make justice visible in the land, to destroy the wicked person and the evil-doer, so that the strong might not injure the weak" ("Code of Hammurabi," 2009). With that being said, one would imagine that Hammurabi's code would be strictly "an eye for an eye" but the code was more complex than that. Hammurabi wanted to create a framework for justice while protecting the weak but the complex code distinguished punishments between the wealthy or noblemen, the lower-class or commoners, and the slaves. Hammurabi's own words describe this point and the inequality of people under his rule: "If a man has destroyed the eye of a man of the gentleman class, they shall destroy his eye .... If he has destroyed the eye of a commoner ... he shall pay one mina of silver. If he has destroyed the eye of a gentleman's slave ... he shall pay half the slave's price" ("Hammurabi's code: An eye for an eye," n.d.).

When looking at the Code of Hammurabi with respect to the death penalty, there were upwards of 25 crimes punishable by death. These crimes ranged from theft of property from a place of worship or a palace, to providing refuge to an escapee slave (Pickup, 2018). Ironically, murder was excluded from the list of crimes punishable by death. Interestingly, the death penalty also enforced rules to avoid false accusations for criminal offenses by instead enforcing punishment by death of the accuser, if the accused was found not to be guilty of the crime. The code of Hammurabi outlines this idea as it states that, "if anyone bring an accusation of any crime before the elders, and does not prove what he was charged, he shall, if it be a capital offence charged, be put to death."

It is evident that King Hammurabi and the Babylonians believed in a class based society and that not all people were equal. As a result, whether a guilty individual would be killed for a commiting a crime that was punishable by death was dependent on their class, or the class of the victim.

The Hittite Code

In 14th Century B.C., The Hittite Code was another set of laws that prescribed the death penalty. The laws written in this code can be categorized into eight groups of similar clauses and as such are formulated as case laws. They are outlined by a condition, and a ruling that would follow. Although the code prescribed the death penalty, it also had an aversion for the death penalty and preferred to punish serious offenses with enslavement or forced labour. For instance, murder calls for punishment by compensatory payement in the form of slaves instead of death (Good, 1966).

The Hittite Code reserves the death penalty for crimes of a sexual nature. One such offence that is outlined in the code is quite peculiar and specific. In section 191 the Hittite Code states:

A free man who cohabits with several free women of the same family ("sisters and their mother") commits no offence if the women are in different places. But if they are in the same place and he knows that they are related, it is a capital offence (Good, 1966).

The BC Draconian Code of Athens

Athens is thought of as the birthplace of democracy, which stems back to the institutionalization of the Draconian Code of laws. As we progress through the history of the death penalty, this Code of Laws was established in 7th century BC, and it also prescribed the death penalty for crimes. In fact it prescribed the death penalty for every crime committed. These laws were written in blood, and as you might imagine they were also brutal but they were the first institution of written laws. Before the institution of the Draconian Code laws were oral and they were prescribed by the aristocratic class (Mingren, 2022). As one might imagine, the legal system was unfair and often unjust. The aristocratic class was able to manipulate and also exploit the justice system and the oral laws to benefit themselves. Therefore, the Draconian Code eliminated the often unjust interpretations of these oral laws by the aristocrats.

The Draconian Code as mentioned above, was first written in blood instead of ink on tablets made of wood and although this code could be literally understood the blood may be interpreted as a metaphor for the brutality of the laws. These tablets are thought to have lasted 200 years, and the only other direct record of the laws were chiseled into stone tablets but over centuries the inscriptions have been lost as a result of weathering and exposure to the elements (Mingren, 2022). As a result, other ancient sources have been utilized to gain insight on the Draconian Code.

Plutarch is one of these ancient sources, and he claims that even the theft of an apple or cabbage was an offense punishable by death under the Draconian Code. The Athenian Legislator Draco who wrote the law stated that "small [crimes] deserve that (i.e. death), and I have no higher [punishment] for the greater crimes." So it is no surprise that the Draconian Code itself was first written in blood, and can be seen as a metaphor for the brutality of the laws it outlined."

During the time that the Draconian Code was in effect, the executions of individuals guilty of crimes punishable by death were carried out in one of three ways. The first method was throwing the guilty individual into a deep chasm or pit. The second involved leaving the individual to die of exposure, thirst, and hunger while tied to a wooden board. The third method was death from drinking poison. The philosopher Socrates met his fate with the use of the third method, poison class (Mingren, 2022).

The Roman Law of the Twelve Tablets

In 5th century BC, the Roman Law of the Twelve Tablets is the next instance of laws containing the death penalty that has been recorded in chronological history. During this period, death sentences were carried out by methods such as beheading, boiling in oil, burying individuals alive, burning, crucifixion, stoning, strangling, and being thrown apart amongst others.

Although the various methods of punishment by death may illustrate that the Roman Law of the Twelve Tablets was harsh, it did take into consideration intent to commit the crime when condemning a guilty individual. For example, the law states:

"Any person who destroys by burning any building or heap of corn deposited alongside a house shall be bound, scourged, and put to death by burning at the stake provided that he has committed the said misdeed with malice aforethought; but if he shall have committed it by accident, that is, by negligence, it is ordained that he repair the damage or, if he be too poor to be competent for such punishment, he shall receive a lighter punishment" (Kreis, 2009).

Mosaic Law

The Mosaic Law which is understood to be law given to the Israelites through Moses by God according to the Old Testament. In the Old Testament, the word "law" is used in place of the translation for the Hebrew word, torah, meaning "instruction." The law outlines the ten commandments and includes many rules for religious observance that are seen in the first five books of the Hebrew Bible (Ukuekpeyetan-Agbikimi, 2014). These first five books are commonly known as the Torah, or "the Law." Although this law and the Torah guide the religious practice and personal conduct in non-religious lives of individuals in Judaism, the Mosaic Law also prescribes the death penalty. For this reason, it is a curious thought that the death penalty is included in the Mosaic Law.

Commonly, the Mosaic Law can be divided into three parts for analysis, but this division was not made in the scriptures. The first section is commonly thought of as the "Moral Law" or the Ten Commandments which governed the moral life and and guides Israel in principles of right and wrong in the face of God and man. The second section is referred to as the "Judgements" or the Social Law which governed the secular, social, political, and economic aspects of Israel. The third section would then be the "Ordinances" or the Ceremonial Law that governs religious practice and gives guidance for worship to God. The Ceremonial Law included the guidance for priesthood, the tabernacle, and the sacrifices (Ukuek-peyetan-Agbikimi, 2014).

In ancient Israel the death penalty was the maximum penalty for various crimes, although it was not the mandatory penalty for most crimes. Verses 30-31 of the Mosaic Law state:

"If anyone kills a person, the murderer shall be put to death at the evidence of witnesses, but no person shall be put to death on the testimony of one witness. Moreover, you shall not take ransom for the life of a murderer who is guilty of death, but he shall surely be put to death."

This verse outlines that individuals convicted of murder were executed, but it also implies that payment of ransom or monetary compensation may be an acceptable punishment or fine for crimes other than murder (Leithart, 2019). Tying this back to Judaism, it is believed that God would accept the sacrificial blood of an animal in the place of the blood of a sinner. Therefore, it is possible that an individual guilty of a crime other than murder may accept a lesser penalty than death and God would treat the sin as one that could be atoned for by sacrifice. In ancient Israel, it was the human representatives who governed Israel that sentenced the sinners and accepted their sacrificial atonement.

During this time in ancient Israel, the death penalty was only carried out following a trial and due process in order to protect the rights of citizens and provide the accused with a fair chance to be proven not guilty. As mentioned in verse 30-31, "no person shall be put to death on the testimony of one witness" so the accused must be found guilty through the testimony of two or three witnesses.

The Torah, which treated homosexual acts as sins also criminalized them and states in a commandment to execute a man who lies with a man (Leithart, 2019). Although, this can not be directly translated to killing a homosexual as a result of due process and the need for a trial proceeding punishment by death for the criminal act. In the Mosaic law, adultery was treated much the same as homosexual acts but these two crimes like all others had to be proven by the testimony of two or three witnesses. In the case of sexual crimes this would often be a difficult standard to meet in order for an individual to be punished by death. As mentioned before with crimes other than murder, the representatives of God were able to punish individuals by means other than execution so death was not the mandatory punishment for sexually deviant acts.

Biblical Theology of the Death Penalty

As seen in the Mosaic law, the death penalty can be traced back to biblical theology and in fact it is a foundational principle. In the Garden Adam was told, "from the tree of knowledge of good and evil you shall not eat, for in the day that you eat from it you shall surely die." Although the death sentence was substituted for by the sacrifice of a substitute in the case of Adam and instead a less severe form of death was imposed on Adam based on biblical history. Adam was exiled from the tree of life, and death was still the fundamental principle and curse against those who sinned.

Based on biblical theology, Israel's worship of Judaism based on the Torah was centered around justice of the death penalty through slaughter or sacrifice of a representative or substitutionary animal (Leithart, 2019). In biblical theology it is believed that Jesus accepted this curse on behalf of His people, and that the sacrifice would save them from the threat of death. Therefore, ancient Israel's observation of Judaism based on the Mosaic law allowed for justice of the death penalty in order to support the structure of biblical redemption as was seen with Adam.

The Death Penalty in Britain

Britain has had a strong influence on the colonies, and has a long history of the death penalty. Around 450 BC, individuals were often condemned to death by being thrown into a quagmire but by the 10th century in Britain the most frequented method of execution was hanging from gallows (Reggio, 1999). In the Middle Ages, capital punishment was often also accompanied by forms of torture, especially for the lower class. Some examples of this brutality included being burned for marrying a Jew, beheading the upper class, boiling the guilty, or even pressing for those who would not confess to a crime. In the case of pressing, the executioner would place heavy weights on the victim's chest and on the first day the victim was given a small quantity of bread and the second day a small drink of water, and so on as the days passed until they either confessed or died (Reggio, 1999).

Under the rule of Henry VIII in Britain, the death toll is estimated to be around 72 000 but the number of capital offences only continued to rise until the 1700s (Reggio, 1999). During this time there were 222 crimes that were punishable by means of death and included stealing forty shillings from a house, or five shillings from a shop, counterfeiting tax stamps, or even cutting down a tree (History of the death penalty, 2019). However, it was up to a jury to convict the individuals and oftentimes they strayed from convicting if the penalty was great when the crime was not. It was not until 1823 when laws were passed and reforms took place to remove punishment by death for crimes. From 1823 to 1837 many capital offenses were removed, and in 1840 there was an attempt to abolish all capital punishment but it was not met with success (Reggio, 1999). Continuing through to the nineteenth and twentieth centuries capital offenses continued to be removed as punishment for crimes in Britain, as well as other countries in Europe but it was still not completely abolished.

Early Instances of the Death Penalty

The first historically recorded instance of the death penalty occurred in 16th century BC Egypt where a member of nobility was accused of performing magic, and was ordered to take his own life. During this time, the non-nobility would usually be killed with an axe. In the English American colonies the first recorded execution was in 1608 when George Kendall of Virginia was punished by death after being accused of plotting to betray the British to the Spanish (Reggio, 1999). Soon after in 1612 the governor of Virginia, Sir Thomas Dale, enacted the Divine, Moral, and Martial Laws that enforced the death penalty for offenses as minor as stealing grapes, or killing animals without permission. These laws were harsh and as a result they only lasted until 1619 when they were softened in hopes that settlers would be more willing to move to Virginia.

Throughout the 17th century, many colonies employed the death penalty but while some were strict in their use of it, others were less so. For instance, in Massachusetts Bay the first documented execution was in 1630 but at this time there were no capital statutes in place. Many of the early laws put in place by the colonies during this time were also accompanied by Scripture from the Old Testament to utilize biblical theology as the basis of these laws (Reggio, 1999).

History of the Death Penalty in America

In the United States of America, there are currently 31 out of the 50 states that still employ the death penalty today. Although not all of them still employ its practice as 11 of those states have not sentenced an individual to death in over a decade (Pickup, 2018). Robert Dunham, the executive director of the Death Penalty Information Center (DPIC) has stated that, "we are witnessing a significant decline in the use of the death penalty, and it's a long-term decline." With that being said, there are still around 3000 individuals on death row, but the country is moving closer to abolition.

The death penalty in America can be traced back to Britain as the practice of capital punishment was brought by British settlers in the age of discovery ("Early history of the death penalty," n.d.). Captain George Kendall who was accused of spying on the British for the Spanish was the first instance of the death penalty being executed in the "new world." As a result, many blame the British for the existence of the death penalty in the Americas and it was in 1776 that reforms of the death penalty were first made in America. Interestingly, this was at the same time that 13 American colonies that were at war with Britain regarded themselves as sovereign states with the Declaration of Independence.

The Death Penalty in Canada

Capital punishment was documented as early as 1749 in Halifax when Peter Catcel, a sailor, was convicted for killing a man. He was found guilty before the general court of Halifax's governor and six accompanying councilors and was hanged two days later (Gendreau & Renke, 2020).

In pre-confederation Canada there were hundreds of crimes that were punishable by death. Before 1859, Canada was known as British North America and operated under British law so the history of the death penalty in Canada can also be traced back to British influence ("Death Penalty in Canada," n.d.). During this time, British North America had around 230 offences that were punishable by death and some of these included peculiar crimes such as being found disguised in a forest. By 1865, the only crimes considered punishable by death were murder, treason, and rape.

In 1962 at the Don jail in Toronto, Ronald Turpin and Arther Lucas were the last prisoners that were executed in Canada since 1859 (CLÉMENT, n.d.). Under prime minister John Diefenbaker all death sentences were then converted to life imprisonment from 1963 onwards and in 1976 the death penalty was only utilized for individuals of the Armed Forces that were found to be guilty of cowardice, desertion, unlawful surrender, or spying for an enemy. In 1998, the federal government in Canada made the decision to abolish state executions (CLÉMENT, n.d.).

References

Gendreau, P., & Renke, W. (2020). Capital Punishment in Canada. In *The Canadian Encyclopedia.*

Good, E. M. (1966). Capital punishment and its alternatives in Ancient Near Eastern Law. Stan. L. Rev., 19, 947.

Kreis, S. (2009, August 03). The Laws of the Twelve Tables, c.450 B.C.

Leithart, P. (2019, June 06). The death penalty in the Mosaic Law.

Mingren, W. (2022, April 11). Brutal draconian laws of ancient Greece were etched in blood.

Pickup, O. (2018, September 09). Exploring the complicated history of the death penalty.

Reggio, M. H. (1999, February 9). History of the death penalty.

Ukuekpeyetan-Agbikimi, N.A. (2014, July) The Mosaic Law and Conflict Resolution. Global Journal of Arts Humanities and Social Sciences., Vol.2, No.5, pp. 97-107.

3

Mythology of the Death Penalty

by Benjamin A. Turner

✚

The death penalty frequently plays a significant role in mythology due to the significance and finality of the matter. When an authority determines that a person must die either out of some collective need or as strictly a punitive measure, it can reflect on the powers held by that authority. To begin with; particularly in cases where the authority is commonly believed to have been wrong or overbearing in its application of the death penalty, movements can be cemented and the person executed is frequently raised to mythological status in the popular imagination.Myth is a symbolic narrative, frequently but not always overtly religious in nature, often involving real people who were involved in extraordinary events or circumstances. The subjects of myth are often portrayed as being superhuman for their acts (Britannica, nd.).

This chapter will examine the mythological status achieved by three famously executed individuals including Socrates, Guy Fawkes, and José Rizal. All three of these individuals achieved a sort of mythological status after their deaths, all three were put to death by governments fearful of their ideas and/or actions, and all three became symbols for the independence of thought and action in subsequent years.

Socrates

Socrates was a philosopher who lived in Athens, ancient Greece and remains one of the most influential thinkers in Western philosophy, his thoughts and methods were so influential in fact that some argue his lasting impact may be as great as figures including Jesus, Buddha, or Muhammad (Koslicki & Harris, 2019). His life and works inspired young Athenians, some of whom had the great privilege of being taught by Socrates; the most notable of whom is arguably the philosopher Plato (Blyth, 2000). His community saw a tremendous positive impact from his work, but arguably the greatest would be his passion for passing that work on to younger generations.

The city-state of Athens was one of the earliest democracies in Europe, although their form of democracy bears little resemblance to the current liberal democratic model that is commonly found. Socrates had complicated political views, and while he was a reformer with regard to traditional power structures and the unquestioning adherence to religious custom over logical analysis (Koslicki & Harris, 2019), he was also critical of the desirability of democracy in matters of governance. Socrates enjoyed celebrity status for many years, although his ideas were controversial it was difficult to argue with him. The status and influence he had were at one time quite substantial, but his controversial nature was also his ultimate undoing. In 399 BCE Socrates was put on trial by an Athenian jury consisting of 500 citizens for the crime of impiety (Koslicki & Harris, 2019). More precisely, he was charged with corrupting young people, inventing new divinities, and not recognizing the gods of the city.

Socrates possessed an almost fanatical dedication to virtue and truth, part of that commitment was to be an upstanding, law-abiding citizen; additionally, he had an obligation to Apollo to continue his mission in Athens if possible (Blyth, 2000). These commitments obliged Socrates to participate in his trial, to do his best to mount a valid defense to obtain an acquittal from the jury; in a heavy note of irony, however, Socrates was guilty of the crimes brought against him from the perspective of his opposition and he knew it. He would not have believed that his actions were unjust or immoral, but he was left to attempt to convince the jury that he was innocent of having done things he did indeed do, which put his various commitments to truth and virtue in conflict with one another (Blyth, 2000).

To further contribute to the irony, Socrates was first offered the option to enter voluntary exile and opted instead to go to trial (Britannica, nd). It was his decision to sit and be judged by a jury of Athenian citizens, who in his mind were not fit to make judgements of him. And again after his conviction, he had the opportunity to propose an alternative sentence to death, which he declined (Britannica, nd). Finally, he also refused an opportunity to escape captivity because it was inconsistent with his commitment to never do anything wrong, he would be disrespecting the law and damaging the reputations of family and friends (Britannica, nd). So strong was his commitment to his virtues that he refused to accept exile, propose a more reasonable sentence, or take advantage of an opportunity to escape because in his mind he had done nothing wrong. His personal conviction was that when presented with an impossible situation he should not violate his values, rather he should stand and face the accusations and do his best to present his actions for what he viewed them to be.

Accounts of his testimony at the trial support this point, Blyth (2000) suggests that Socrates actually treated the trial as an intellectual exercise and regarded the jurors as students. All through the trial he regarded the jurors with an improper title, only assigning the formally correct title after the verdict was handed down and even then only treating the jurors that had voted to acquit him with the customary respect (Blyth, 2000). He opened his defense by asking the jurors to disregard his manner of speaking, and instead to focus on whether the case itself is just. When answering the charge of impiety and corruption, he points to his devoted service to Apollo as evidence that he is in fact extremely pious. In discussing whether he has corrupted young people he asserts the benefit that his influence has had on the city over the years as evidence he has enlightened them (Blyth, 2000). Throughout the trial Socrates appeared to be less defending himself and more testing the abilities of the jury, to be presenting them with the challenge of coming out with the correct verdict based on logic as he defined it (Blyth, 2000).

At one point in the trial, he famously exclaimed that "the unexamined life is not worth living" (Britannica, nd). This was a central point in his criticism of democracy, but more broadly as an expression of the tragedy of humanity that so many people go through life knowing only what they have been told, failing to question or think for themselves. To Socrates, if even one of his 500 jurors was living an unexamined life or failed to consider the implications of the trial, then the entire process was unjust. It was not enough to simply go through life trying to mind one's own business and not do any harm, one also is required to examine their actions harshly and consider all the consequences therein. An excellent contemporary example would be the common practice of people in Canada to purchase a cup of coffee at the drive-thru every morning on their way to work. In an unexamined life this is a harmless action, or perhaps even has a net positive value because the transaction stimulates economic activity. But when millions of people start their day by purchasing coffee in a disposable cup with a plastic lid it creates an environmental catastrophe. Did the individual intend harm when they purchased the coffee? Is the

40

impact of their one cup significant? To Socrates, the lack of intention does not mean the action is not harmful, and even making a small contribution to a large problem is still wrong. His extreme interpretation of his values put Socrates in an impossible situation; to be faced with unjust charges, judged by an unqualified jury, and found guilty for actions that should not have been crimes in the first place from his perspective.

This stubborn insistence on strictly following a moral code proved fatal to Socrates. What's more, his cause of death is recorded as hemlock poisoning (Koslicki & Harris, 2019). Hemlock was a common method of execution in ancient Greece, where the person condemned to die is allowed to take their own life. Socrates further proved his commitment to his virtues by carrying out his death sentence himself. The culmination of these factors related to his trial in combination with the greater impact of his life's work firmly placed Socrates in the realm of mythology, to be forever remembered for his logic and virtues, and the seemingly superhuman adherence to those values to the point of carrying out his own execution in accordance with the court's decision.

Guy Fawkes

The gunpowder plot of 1605 by Guy Fawkes and a group of co-conspirators resulted in the trial and executions of all participants, most famously Guy Fawkes (Fraser, 2002). The result of the plot was that the following year a new holiday was created in London called Guy Fawkes Night, Guy Fawkes Day, Plot Night, and Bonfire Day. It was to be a day of thanksgiving and joy at the deliverance of King James I from the assassination plot. To mark the occasion bonfires were to be lit and accompanied by fireworks, and sometime later the burning of effigies was added to the tradition. Figures traditionally burned include Guy Fawkes and the Pope (Fraser, 2002).

Popular rhymes were made up to commemorate the event, perhaps the most famous being

"Remember, remember, the Fifth of November
Gunpowder treason and plot;
I see no reason why Gunpowder treason
Should ever be forgot.
A stick and a stake
For King George's sake!" (Burne, 1912, pp 411).

Guy Fawkes grew up in England under the Anglican church, but converted to Christianity as a young man and migrated to mainland Europe where he enlisted with the catholic Spanish to fight against the protestant Dutch reformers in the 80 years war (Fraser, 2002). This alone was viewed as a criminal act at the time, Fawkes would have been considered in open rebellion against the Crown. It is doubly true since England and Spain were at war with each other at the time, although no land engagements had taken place at the time. When the war ended, Fawkes returned to England and began plotting with his co-conspirators to assassinate King James I to advance their goal of placing a Catholic on the throne (Fraser, 2002). He was put in charge of the gunpowder cache the group had stockpiled in a chamber beneath the House of Lords, and on the 5th of November 1605 was caught guarding the explosive powder (Fraser, 2002).

After his capture, Fawkes was tortured by members of the King's Privy chamber but was defiant. He gave his name as John Johnson, and at one point when asked what he was doing with so much gunpowder gave the snide answer that he was intending to blow the Scotch beggars back to the mountains. His manner in the early hours of his interrogation actually earned him the admiration of the King.

Admiration did not prevent the King from ordering Fawkes to be tortured to reveal the names of his co-conspirators, authorizing a steadily escalating treatment until the prisoner broke (Fraser, 2002). He was transferred to the Tower of London to be interrogated further and tortured, revealing his identity and plans on the 7th of November; Fawkes stated his motive was to advance the interests of catholicism and save his immortal soul. The following day on the 8th of November he began to give up the names of his accomplices (Fraser, 2002).

The trial took place on the 27th of January,1606. Fawkes was tried with seven of his accomplices at Westminster Hall where the entire group was found guilty of high treason. The sentence was an elaborate death, involving being drawn backwards by a horse, having their genitals cut off and burned, and their bowels and hearts removed. Finally, the prisoners were to be decapitated and the dismembered parts of their bodies displayed as a warning to others who might wish to commit similar crimes as they serve as prey for the birds (Fraser, 2002). Fawkes, possibly by accident but likely intentionally, fell from the scaffold when he was called up for execution, breaking his neck in the process and saving him the agony of his assigned mode of death. As per tradition, his corpse was still mutilated in the prescribed manner and the pieces of him were shipped to various parts of the Kingdom for display (Fraser, 2002). The place Fawkes earned in the mythology of the death penalty is dissimilar from that of Socrates, although he demonstrated similar resolve. But while the execution of Socrates is a symbol of independence and the tyranny of an overbearing state, Guy Fawkes Day is a celebration of the triumph of the state over treachery. It has remained a celebration of the state for hundreds of years as detailed by Carey (1908) and Burne (1912). More recently, thanks to the popular graphic novel *V for Vendetta* (Moore & Lloyd, 1988) Guy Fawkes is presented as a hero of certain ideals of modern liberalism, a symbol of sacrifice in the face of an overbearing and unjust state. This appropriation of Fawkes deepens the mythology of the man, and while it is true he was fighting against an establishment that had largely criminalized his faith, he was not fighting for broad religious freedom. At best, Fawkes was fighting for his own religious freedom, but he had little interest in the freedom of others unless they were catholic. To put it simply, Fawkes was just as oppressive and fanatical as the crown, he simply belonged to a different church.

One common element of mythology is the distortion of the original events to serve a contemporary message or set of values, and precisely this phenomenon has clearly occurred with the mythology around Guy Fawkes.

José Rizal

The final figure we will discuss in this chapter is José Rizal, informally the national hero of the Philippines. During the Spanish colonial period of that country, his writings inspired the independence movement that would eventually result in Philippine independence. He was arrested, tried, and executed by Spanish colonial officials after the start of the revolutionary war despite having had no part in planning or participating in the rebellion; nevertheless, his ideas helped start the war and his goals were aligned with the revolutionaries. It is also important to note here that Rizal was a strong advocate for nonviolent measures.

In being the inspiration for the Philippine revolution, Rizal is regarded popularly as the national hero of the Philippines and is thus afforded mythological status in the character of the nation. An example of this can be seen in Manila at the site of his execution, there is a set of brass footprints set into the ground leading up to the spot where Rizal was killed, denoting his final steps.

As a young man, he travelled to Europe and visited many old and great independent nations, and was likely inspired by what he saw in the freedoms and self-determination enjoyed by the populations of Spain, Belgium, Germany, and France in the late 19th century.

He published *Dimanche des Rameaux*, a socio-political essay in Berlin in 1886, and was interviewed by German police shortly thereafter because they suspected he might be a French spy. In truth, his writing was a discussion of the importance of Palm Sunday (Zaide & Zaide, 1957).

Rizal's two most famous novels, *Noli Me Tángere* and *El Filibusterismo* were controversial with Spanish colonial officials and the upper classes of Filipino society because they are critical of the structure of Filipino society under colonial rule, particularly with regard to the power of the church. Rizal returned to Manila in 1892 where he formed a small social advocacy group attempting through peaceful means to achieve modest reforms; the movement was disbanded by the governor, largely because of Rizal's affiliation with the group because he had been declared an enemy of the state as a consequence of his earlier publications (Zaide & Zaide, 1957).

He lived for several years in exile within the Philippines, and through connections with local Jesuit missionaries was eventually allowed to return to Manila. His trouble was far from over, however. In 1896 he was arrested and charged with rebellion, the war of independence was in full swing and the Spanish were rapidly losing control of their colony. Rizal was found guilty because his writings had been instrumental to the birth of the rebellion, and he was executed by firing squad on the 30th of December, 1896 (Zaide & Zaide, 1957).

The execution of Rizal did not prevent the eventual Spanish loss of their colony, although just as the rebellion was nearing the end of the war Spain sold the colony to the United States which intervened and put in place a new regime that was successfully adopted by the people. Following his death and the political reorganization of the Philippines, Rizal only became a stronger figure in the national identity of Filipinos, achieving martyr status for having given his life to the cause (Valenzuela, 2014). He was a popular figure in life, and in death, he has become an important symbol of nationalism for more than 100 years. Unlike Fawkes, the legacy of Rizal remains relatively true to his initial intentions. So firm is his place in the national imagination that Rizal is the image in profile on the backside of one peso coin in the Philippines, and there are banks, universities, insurance companies, sports arenas and all other manners of culturally significant institutions named after him (Francia, 2014). To this day every town square in the nation has a statue of his likeness prominently featured (Francia, 2014).

Conclusion

The death penalty has significant cultural power all over the world, and often when governments intend to silence a dissenter by executing them it has precisely the opposite effect; they may instead create a martyr who is remembered for their sacrifice to their cause and becomes an inspiration for hundreds or even thousands of years as is the case with José Rizal and Socrates respectively. In other cases the legacy of the executed may be more complicated, the state might successfully create a popular national whipping boy as England did with Guy Fawkes for almost four centuries, though it is noteworthy that the legacy of Fawkes has been co-opted in recent decades in service of more contemporary values.

Such is the risk of executing a political dissident, it is difficult for the state to ensure the correct messaging is maintained. The death of a dissident today often creates a powerful symbol of opposition tomorrow that is far more durable and long-lived than the living person ever could have aspired to be. And sometimes a martyr enjoys such high status and regard as to be elevated into mythology, where the actual intentions and values they represented in the first place are less important than the name recognition paired with a contemporary narrative. Myths are often by their very nature a gross distortion of the truth.

References

Beck, E. (1984). Children's Guy Fawkes Customs in Sheffield. Folklore, 95(2), 191–203. _

Blyth, D. (2000). Socrates' Trial and Conviction of the Jurors in Plato's Apology. Philosophy & Rhetoric, 33(1), 1–22. _

Britannica. (n.d.). Myth. Encyclopedia Britannica.

Britannica. (n.d.). Why didn't Socrates try to escape his death sentence? Encyclopedia Britannica.

Burne, C. S. (1912). Guy Fawkes' Day. *Folklore*, 23(4), 409–426.

Carey, E. H. (1908). The Fifth of November and Guy Fawkes. Folklore, 19(1), 104–105.

Francia, L. (2014). *José Rizal: A Man for All Generations*. The Antioch Review, 72(1), 44–60. _

Fraser, A. (2002). *The gunpowder plot: Terror faith in 1605*. Phoenix.

Koslicki, K., & Harris, J. P. (2019). Introduction to "Death of a Gadfly: An Interdisciplinary Examination of the Trial and Execution of Socrates." Mouseion: Journal of the Classical Association of Canada, 15(3), 341–346.

Moore, A., Lloyd, D. (1988). V for Vendetta. DC Comics.

The Virgin Warrior: The Life and Death of Joan of Arc. (2010). Contemporary Review, 292(1697), 263.

Valenzuela, M. T. (2014). Constructing national heroes: postcolonial Philippine and Cuban biographies of Jose Rizal and Jose Marti. Biography, 37(3), 745.

Zaide, G., & Zaide, S. (1957). José Rizal. life, works, and writings, etc. with a portrait. Manila.

4

Evolution of Execution

by Irene Falade

✣

Throughout the long history of the death penalty, the execution methods that have been used to enforce the capital punishment have constantly changed and evolved according to the eras and justice systems in power at said times. The oldest record of the death penalty laws was found in the Code of King Hammurabi of Babylon which dates back to 18th century B.C. (FindLaw, 2019). These records were in the form of stone tablets dubbed as The Hammurabi Code and it detailed the punishment of death penalty for 25 different crimes, some as minor as theft and perjury (FindLaw, 2019). During this time, there were many different execution methods that could be used to carry out the penalty, and it varied based on factors such as one's social status (FindLaw, 2019). As society progressed and developed into the modern era, methods of execution also began to change and become limited to more humane, less torturous approaches (Crime Museum, n.d.). In this chapter, we will be discussing the various changes in society's approach to execution according to their different eras, as well as taking a closer look at Canada's execution methods prior to abolition and the approach taken by the military when it comes to enforcing the death penalty among its forces.

The Early Eras B.C

Although the death penalty laws are noted to have existed since as far back as the 18th century B.C. in the Code of King Hammurabi of Babylon, the earliest record of a death sentence being carried out was not till the 16th century B.C. in Egypt (Reggio, n.d.). The record reported that the death sentence was carried out for a noble man who had been accused of using magic, the execution method ordered was for the culprit to commit suicide (Reggio, n.d.). Suicide is the act of intentionally seeking to taking one's own life (Merriam-Webster, n.d.). According to Reggio (n.d.) this method of execution was only reserved for nobility at the time, while non-nobility sentenced to death were killed with an axe. In these ancient times, there were many other various methods of execution enforced to carry out the death penalty for wrongdoers. These death sentences in the 18th century B.C., 14th century B.C., 7th century B.C, 5th century B.C. etc., to name a few stand out years, were implemented by way of crucifixion, drowning, impalement, burning alive, beating to death, stoning and even burial alive (Crime Museum, n.d., Death Penalty Information Center, n.d., Reggio, n.d.).

Crucifixion

As written by Retief and Cilliers (2003), crucifixion is said to be a cruel and shameful manner of death. Its origins are not certain but it is assumed to have originated from Assyrians and Babylonians but was most frequently used by Persians in 6th century B.C. (Retief & Cillier, 2003). Then it was brought to Eastern Mediterranean countries by Alexander the Great in the 4th century B.C. shortly afterwards in the 3rd century B.C., the Phoenicians introduced crucifixion to the Romans (Retief & Cillier, 2003). The Romans perfected the method of crucifixion for 500 years before its abolishment by Constantine the First in 4th century A.D. (Retief & Cillier, 2003). The Romans made use of this execution method for slaves, Christians, disgraced soldiers and foreigners, but it was a method they rarely ever used on roman citizens (Retief & Cillier, 2003).

According to Retief and Cilliers (2003), the execution method of crucifixion is one where a person is hanged by their arms on a cross or similar structure until death. Earlier forms of crucifixion frequently used in Persia had the victim tied to a tree or a post and in some cases impaled on a post, with their feet not touching the ground (Retief & Cillier, 2003). The use of a cross in the process of crucifixion was brought into popular use by the Romans, and more than the well-known Latin cross, there were other types of crosses used such as viz, an X-shaped cross, and the Tua cross that is capital T shaped (Retief & Cillier, 2003).

In the process of crucifixion, Retief and Cilliers (2003) state that in Roman law, people given the death penalty had to be scourged first but women, Roman soldiers or senators were exempted from this procedure. Scourging was an act where the culprit was stripped naked, tied to a standing post and flogged with use of wooden staves or short whips with leather thongs that had small balls or sharp sheep bone fragments tied to it (Retief & Cillier, 2003). Roman law assigned no limits to the extent of the victim's flogging and it was usually done in order to weaken them, sometimes the victim even died during the process (Retief & Cillier, 2003). For surviving victims, they are taunted by bystanders and made to carry their cross to their execution place (Retief & Cillier, 2003). Once they arrived, Retief and Cilliers (2003) state that according to the customs of Jerusalem, women would give the victim a pain-relieving drink of wine and myrrh or incense. The victim was then stripped, laid on the cross with their arms stretched out on either side to be tied or nailed to the cross by their wrists (Retief & Cillier, 2003). The cross and victim were then raised to an upright position with the victim's feet tied or nailed down (Retief & Cillier, 2003). Soldiers were instructed to wait by the cross until the victim's death which usually took from 3-4 hours to 3-4 days (Retief & Cillier, 2003).

Drowning

In Ancient Rome, there was a very specific punishment for parricides, which meant the murder of ones' own parents (Reggio, n.d.). This punishment was called *Poena Cullei*, latin for "punishment of the sack", it involved the victim being put into a leather sack along with a snake, a rooster, a monkey and a dog to be drowned (Egmond, 1995, p.159). The reason behind this special execution method was that the Romans took the murder of one's own parent as an act against nature and a sign of ungratefulness, not being filial (M.ADMIN, n.d.). The *Poena Cullei* was mainly used during the 15th, 16th and early 17th century B.C. in Rome, however according to Egmond (1995) the execution method was also found in German speaking countries between 1200 and the middle of the 18th century, where it was referred to as Sãcken (p.159-160).

Egmond (1995) states that the process of the *Poena Cullei* according to Roman ritual involved the culprit being taken to their execution place on a cart pulled by black oxen and flogged with special rods called the *virgae sanguineae* (p.166). At the arrival at the execution place, the criminal had their head covered with a cap made of wolf's skin dubbed the *folliculus lupinus* in Latin, and their feets tied to wooden soles (Egmond, 1995, p.166). Then they were bundled up in a leather sack along with four live animals; a cock, a dog, a snake and a monkey before being drowned together (Egmond, 1995, p.166). According to Egmond (1995), this form of capital punishment faded out of existence along with the Roman empire before being brought back for use in German territories (p.166). Unlike the Roman ritual process, the Germans did not flog the culprit or tie their feet to wooden soles, their heads with a cap or any of the pre-drowning rituals, they simply put the person into the leather bag with the four live animals and drowned them (Egmond, 1995, p.166). This method of execution was last used in

18th century Germany before fading out of existence once again (Egmond, 1995, p.159).

Stoning

The origins of stoning as a capital punishment for those sentenced to death is difficult to trace because it an execution method that is as old as the Bible's Old Testament (Beccia, 2021). It is said that stoning has been found to have some roots in Ancient Greece and Judeo-Christian religious texts, it has also been referenced in the Torah, which is the compilation of the first five books in the Hebrew bible (NBC News, 2010, Saunders, 2019). Stoning as an execution method is usually reserved for people who commit adultery, namely women, but it also has history in being used to execute people for homosexuality, prostitution, murder and blasphemy (NBC News, 2010, Beccia, 2021). The way it works is that those sentenced to death by stoning are buried in a hole and covered with soil, for women they are covered up to their necks while men are covered up to their waists (NBC News, 2010). This procedure was apparently set by Article 102 of the Islamic Penal Code, which also states that should the person buried be able to dig themselves out of the hole they would go unpunished (NBC News, 2010). This was a rare occurrence however as the hands were also buried alongside the individual and for women who were buried up to their necks, there has been no record of any success in escaping (Beccia, 2021, NBC News, 2010). Stoning was considered as a form of community justice in the Muslim world, so a selected group of people were chosen to execute the accused by throwing stones specified in Sharia Law to make sure that the accused does not die too fast or too slow (NBC News, 2010). According to Beccia (2021), stoning is still in use in today's capital punishment in certain parts of the world such as, Pakistan, northern Nigeria, Saudi Arabia, Somalia, Sudan, the United Arab Emirates, Qatar, Mauritania, and Yemen. And a more recent use of stoning for execution was found in 2019 where the Sultan of Brunei proclaimed that a death sentence by stoning would be enforced for muslims found guilty of adultery or homosexuality (Beccia, 2021).

Socrates

Socrates was a famous Greek philosopher that was given the death sentence in the year 399 B.C. in Athens, Greece (Islam & Mahabarata, 2020). This was the most notorious execution in the B.C. era (Reggio, n.d.). Socrates was found guilty of corrupting the youth, refusing to recognize the gods of the state and introducing new gods, this was an unforgivable crime during its time (Islam & Mahabarata, 2020). The execution method according to Athenian laws of the time was the drinking of a cup of hemlock, a poisonous plant (Islam & Mahabarata, 2020). In other words Socrates was sentenced to a death penalty suicide. The hemlock plant is very toxic and deadly once ingested by humans or animals, the symptoms develop very quickly as well (Christopher, 2020). The death of Socrates is detailed by his student Plato in his popular dialogue writing from the Middle Ages, Phaedo (Islam & Mahabarata, 2020). Plato describes the scene,

> "After drinking the poison, he (Socrates) was ordered to walk around until his legs felt numb. After he lay down, a man placed his hand on Socrates' body and for a moment examined his leg, then pinched his leg hard and asked if he felt it. Socrates said 'no' and then after that, the numbness crept into his thighs and the rest of his upper body. His face showed us that Socrates was cold and stiff. And again the man touched him and said that when he reached his heart, Socrates would die. The cold has now reached the area around the groin and opened his face which has been covered. These are Socrates' last words. ; Crito, we owe Asclepius the chicken. Please, don't forget to pay the debt" (Islam & Mahabarata, 2020).

The Middle Ages

Execution methods used to carry out death penalties in the Middle Ages were quite numerous, similar to that of the time before it, the justice systems developed various options to execute guilty parties. Some of these methods were taken from older empires and cultures and further developed, while others were the first of their kind seeing such frequent use. These execution methods ranged from hanging which became the staple execution process in 10th century A.D. Britain, to the bloody 16th century reign of Henry VIII that implemented boiling, burning at the stake, beheading, and drawing and quartering (Death Penalty Information Center, n.d.).

Hanging

Hanging is not only one of the oldest, but it is also one of the most widely used execution methods in enforcing the death penalty. And unlike other earlier execution methods, hanging is still being used all over the modern world (Crime Museum, n.d.). It was frequently used in Ancient Rome for executions under their laws before being obtained by the Anglo-Saxons from their Germanic ancestors (Britannica, 2020). More well-known is the fact that hangings were the go-to execution method for people who committed homicide in 12th century England and then later culprits of any felonies (Britannica, 2020). Aside from its use in the British Empire, hangings were also used in places that adopted the Anglo-American common law and then later Russia, Austria, Hungary, Japan and many other parts of the world (Britannica, 2020). Hangings were also known to be the regular method of execution in the United States up until the 20th century (Britannica, 2020).

With how widespread hanging is as a means of execution, its procedure has been adapted across different times, nations and cultures (Crime Museum, n.d.). Hanging by its definition according to Britannica (2020), is death by strangling or breaking of a person's neck by a suspended noose. The traditional method of this manner of execution had the victims hanged from the gallows as seen in 10th century Britain, or a crossbeam until their death by asphyxiation (Britannica, 2020, Reggio, n.d.).

This traditional method now termed, "the short drop" hanging, was in frequent use for decades until the 19th century (Mukunth, 2020). The process of the short drop hanging according to Mukunth (2020), was that a noose is placed around the neck of the victim while they stood upon a short structure such as a stool. With the noose in place, the support is then kicked out of the way, leaving the victim to slowly strangle to death from the short drop (Mukunth, 2020). How this leads to death is due to the noose squeezing on the carotid artery that carries blood to the brain, it also presses down on the trachea bringing oxygen to the lungs slowing that process (Mukunth, 2020). This causes the blood supply to drop, brain swelling that it presses on the top of the spinal column and pinches on the vagal nerve before finally stopping the victim's heart (Mukunth, 2020). Mukunth (2020) states that, during this slow process the victim would have been unconscious in the first 20 seconds and dead by 20 minutes in.

In more recent years, there has been a switch from the traditional short drop hangings to a more modern form called the "long drop" hanging (Layton & Holt, 2021). This new procedure referred to as "humane hanging" came about in 1866 by an Irish mathematician, science writer and doctor called Samuel Haughton (Layton & Holt, 2021, Mukunth, 2020). Haughton (1866) claimed that the short drop method was too savage and painful to the criminal in a time where science was more advanced (p.8). In his process of developing a modification to the short drop method, Haughton found that there were 3 specific ways hanging resulted in death for an individual (Mukunth, 2020). First was through apoplexy, which is due to pressure on the jugular veins, second was by asphyxia, the stoppage of the windpipe and third was the shock of the medulla oblongata which is the result of a fracture of the vertebral column (Mukunth, 2020). According to Mukunth (2020), Haughton's long drop procedure was developed by knowledge of the fracture of the vertebral column due to shock of the medulla oblongata. The basics behind the long drop was simply that the victim would be dropped from a greater height causing the rope to pull tight and break their neck rather than strangulating them slowly (Mukunth, 2020). The calculations to ensure this method succeeded was that the rope had to be between 4 to 6 feet and the length used during hanging executions needed to achieve a drop energy of 1,708 joules so the victim is not decapitated (Mukunth, 2020). Haughton's long drop was later refined by British executioner William Marwood who decided that the calculations for the long drop needed to take into account the accused's height and weight (Layton & Holt, 2021, Mukunth, 2020). Layton and Holt (2021), add that with the "ideal long drop", the victim's neck is broken, spine severed, their blood pressure drops to zero and they lose consciousness. This is followed by a quick brain death occurring within minutes and a final death that can take up to 20 minutes, during this whole process the victim is unconscious and unable to feel any pain, hence the term "humane hanging" (Layton & Holt, 2021). On the other hand, a "less-than ideal long drop", occurs when the distance of the drop or another factor is miscalculated causing the person to either be decapitated in case of being too long or strangulated in case of being too short (Layton & Holt, 2021).

Boiling Alive

The execution method of being boiled to death was exceptionally cruel and brutal, it was slow and torturous, making it one of the worst ways to die in the Middle Ages (Margaritoff, 2020). Before the Middle Ages, during the time of the Roman empire when Emperor Nero reigned, the penalty of being boiled to death was used to execute thousands of Christians (Margaritoff, 2020). And when the middle ages finally came around, boiling to death as an execution method was made into a legislative penalty in 1531 by Henry VIII (Abbott, 2007, Reggio, n.d.). According to Abbott (2007), King Henry VIII implemented this penalty for poisoning one's husband or master, which he deemed as a form of treason. The process of boiling to death was said to be a very slow process (Margaritoff, 2020). This execution method made use of a large cauldron or container where one of these liquids are heated up; water, oil, molten lead, wax, tallow, or wine (Abbott, 2007). The criminal is placed into the cauldron or container with the boiling hot liquid and left to die excruciatingly (Abbott, 2007). According to Margaritoff (2020), their limbs were the first to burn, as their outer layers such as skin cooked in the liquid, their organs were next. The fluids in the criminal's body also began to boil until they finally died and according to Reggio (n.d.), there are records of some people being boiled for up to two hours before their deaths (Margaritoff, 2020).

Margaritoff (2020) states that one of the only possible ways for the victim to get a quicker death is if the liquid was already boiling prior to them being dropped in. Another way the victim could get a quicker death is by putting their head underneath the liquid to allow their brain to boil (Margaritoff, 2020). This torturous method of execution was also used in 13th to 16th century France and Germany for the crime of "coining" or "clipping, which is explained by Abbott (2007) as, scraping fragments from old coins and melting them to create new coins. However once the minting of coins with milled edges came into practice, it became easier for the authorities to decipher which coins were fake or real, and so the death penalty of boiling a person to death fell out of use (Margaritoff, 2020).

Beheading

Beheading also referred to as decapitation is an execution method that has been used to carry out the death penalty for millennia (New World Encyclopedia, n.d.). It even has various references in biblical records such as John the Baptist who was beheaded after being imprisoned by King Herod (New World Encyclopedia, n.d.). The reason for this was because King Herod had taken Philip, John's brother's wife to marry her and John the Baptist spoke out against it by reprimanding the king's actions (New World Encyclopedia, n.d.). Beheading is just as the name states, in this execution method a person's head is severed from the rest of their body with either an axe or a sword, resulting in instant death (Abbott, 2015). In ancient empires like Greece and Rome, beheading as a capital punishment was viewed as an honourable way to die, hence it was reserved for roman citizens and aristocrats who were warriors and anticipated dying by the sword (Abbott, 2015, New World Encyclopedia, 2020). This belief system was passed down to the Middle Ages and seen in countries like England who reserved beheading as a death penalty for the noblemen because their privilege deemed them as deserving an "honourable" death (New World Encyclopedia, n.d.). When the French revolution came around, beheading was no longer reserved for the nobles or royalty, it became a method of execution that was extended to commoner criminals by use of the guillotine (Abbott, 2015).

According to Abbott (2015), beheading with a sword was only introduced to England in the 11th century by William the Conqueror during his reign. The procedure of a sword beheading had the sentenced criminal standing or kneeling upright as the sword was swung down to take their head (Abbott, 2015). New World Encyclopedia (n.d.) adds that if the axe or sword of the headsman was sharp and his aim true, the decapitation was swift and painless. If the opposite happened where the headsman used a blunt weapon or was clumsy, the decapitation took a few more strikes to fully sever the head (New World Encyclopedia, n.d.). To avoid this scenario, it was apparently advised for the victim to provide the headman with a gold coin prior to their beheading (New World Encyclopedia, n.d). Around the time of the French revolution however, the guillotine was invented and became the common method of beheading criminals with mechanical assistance (New World Encyclopedia, n.d.). The guillotine according to New World Encyclopedia (n.d.) was designed in order to make beheadings quick and painless as well as easier to enforce with little skill. This became the primary method of execution beheadings in France until their death penalty abolition in 1981 (New World Encyclopedia, n.d.).

Burning at Stake

The execution method of burning at the stake was said to have originally been a form of capital punishment in ancient Babylonian times, before later travelling to Europe to be practiced in the Middle ages (Margaritoff, 2020). It was an exceedingly popular punishment method seen in use during the Spanish Inquisition by Spanish heretics and with French martyrs such as the Joan of Arc (Margaritoff, 2020). Burning at the stake was an execution method that was closely tied to the overflowing sexism and superstition of the Mediaeval times (Margaritoff, 2020). According to various sources, getting burned at the stake was a penalty used for accusations of witchcraft and heresy, men found guilty of arson in Germanic Law or 'Mordband' which was a penalty found in the Roman Twelve Tables and bondwomen convicted of stealing under the England Laws of Athelstan (Alchin, 2017, Margaritoff, 2020, Reinhard, 1941, p.186-187). However, the most common and popular use of this capital punishment was for women accused of petty treason, heresy, blasphemy and witchcraft (Margaritoff, 2020). According to Margaritoff (2020), in these times a simple accusation supported by a few others was enough reason for women to be found guilty of sorcery and witchcraft, and in a majority of cases the accusations were put forth by a village rival not the church or authorities.

The process of burning at the stake after a person had been sentenced was that a stake was erected in the chosen execution place and surrounded by a tall pile of straw and wood (Alchin, 2017). There was space left between the stake and the pile for the victim to enter, stripped down and dressed in a shirt covered with sulfur and then chained to the stake (Alchin, 2017). Alchin (2017) adds that more straw and faggots were thrown onto the pile and the accused till they were sufficiently covered and then shortly, they were lit on fire. In some cases to deliver a quick death to the accused, the executioner places opposite the stake, a large iron bar that is breast high which delivers a mortal blow to the accused when the fire is started and spares them the suffering (Alchin, 2017). In other cases, the executioner attaches gunpowder to the victim to explode when heated by the fire and delivering the victim a quicker death, or they would put a chain noose around the victim's neck to strangle them to death while they burned at the stake (Margaritoff, 2020). The punishment of sentencing people to death by burning on the stake for heresy became less popular in the year 1612 but burning people at the stake for other crimes did not completely die out until the 18th century in England (Margaritoff, 2020). Campbell (1984, p.44) states that it was made illegal to burn witches after 1736 but that did not stop the sentencing of women to burning at the stake until the end of the 18th century for petty treason and counterfeiting in the mid 18th century which classified as high treason.

The Modern Era

Compared to the various execution methods used to enforce death penalties in the previous eras, the modern world has come a long way in limiting options for executions. The reason for this development lies in modern society deeming older methods of execution such as hangings, burning at the stake, crucifixion, boiling to death and many more as cruel, unusual forms of punishments, hereby seeking a change for more humane practices of fulfilling the death penalty (Crime Museum, n.d.). The change was even written into the United States Eighth Amendment prohibiting "cruel and unusual punishment" under the law, although it was not officially enforced and made applicable to the states of America until the year 1962 (Bohm, 2007). This meant that the execution methods being used to carry out death sentences prior to that year were not declared cruel and unusual by the supreme court, however they were still believed to be more humane and merciful than earlier methods (Bohm, 2007, Reggio, n.d.). These improved humane methods of executions that are now primarily used in the modern world include, the electric chair, lethal injection, death by firing squad and the gas chamber (Reggio. N.d, Robert, 2007).

Electric Chair

The electric chair also referred to as electrocution is an execution method that was created in 1888 America (Reggio, n.d.). According to Reggio (n.d.) its invention was heavily influenced by the Edison (DC) electric company demonstrating how dangerous its opponent the Westinghouse (AC) electric company could be by electrocuting animals in order to prove that electricity can harm humans too. This led to the creation of the first ever electric chair for enforcing a death sentence by New York city (Reggio, n.d.). The procedure for the electric chair begins with the sentenced prisoner getting their hair shaved mainly from their head, then their entire body is strapped down to the electric chair (Death Penalty Information Center, n.d.). A saline moistened sponge is then placed on their scalp and forehead, followed by the attachment of a metal skull-cap-shaped electrode to the sponge (Death Penalty Information Center, n.d.). According to the Death Penalty Information Center (n.d.), the sponge is soaked in saline to help circulate the electric current in the inmate's body, if it is too wet the electric current gets short-circuited by the saline, and if it's too dry there is a high resistance making it difficult for the current to circulate. The prisoner's leg is also shaved to make room for the attachment of an electrode dampened with conductive jelly before being blindfolded and the room emptied out (Death Penalty Information Center, n.d.). The execution resides in an observation room awaiting the signal from the warden for when it is time to turn on the power supply to the chair (Death Penalty Information Center, n.d.). A high voltage between 500 and 2000 volts is delivered to the prisoner until their heart stops, in cases where they are still alive after the first voltage, more jolts are given until the prisoner is deemed dead (Denno, 2012, Death Penalty Information Center, n.d.). This process is said to last around 2 minutes on average (Denno, 2012). Electrocution became the go-to method of execution in 26 states of America during its peak of popularity in 1949 and by the early 21st century it was one of the two options offered to inmates on death row in multiple states (Denno, 2012). The other option for execution methods was lethal injection and it replaced the electric chair as the most used method of execution during the dawn of the 20th century, and now according to Denno (2012), the electric chair is rarely ever used anymore.

Lethal Injection

Lethal injection is an execution method that was first implemented in the year 1977 by the state of Oklahoma in the U.S (Denno, 2013). This method carried out executions by having the inmates injected with one or more chemicals that resulted in death (Denno, 2013). The first state to carry out the lethal injection in a death sentence was Texas in 1982, executing the convicted Charles Brooks Jr. (Denno, 2013). According to Denno (2013), lethal injection became a widely used and popular execution method, some states in America only relying on it for their executions because it was found to not only be cheaper but also more humane than the electric chair and gas chamber. The first and most common procedure of the lethal injection involved the use of 3 chemicals injected into the inmate through their vein (Denno, 2013). There was a specific order of injections to be followed according to Denno (2013):

(1) sodium thiopental, a barbiturate anesthetic, which is supposed to induce deep unconsciousness in about 20 seconds, (2) pancuronium bromide, a total muscle relaxant that, given in sufficient dosages, paralyzes all voluntary muscles, thereby causing suffocation, and (3) potassium chloride, which induces irreversible cardiac arrest.

Lethal injections were set up this way to cause as little pain and discomfort as possible to the inmates and provide a swift death which usually would take around 5 minutes to complete with death taking place 2 minutes after the final injection is delivered (Denno, 2013). However, like with every other execution method there are cases where the procedure does not go as planned and it results in the prisoner suffering for up to and even more than two hours before they die (Denno, 2013). Denno (2013) claims that some of the botched lethal injection death sentences could possibly be the cause of having uninformed prison personnel and executioners that are not medically trained or qualified, put in charge of the execution process.

In more recent times, there have been constitutional challenges and autopsy evidence that suggest the lethal injection method may not actually be as painless and humane as originally thought (Denno, 2013). According to Caldwell et al. (2020), these findings were spearheaded by Dr. Joel Zivot who had been hired by lawyers of executed prisoners to investigate their autopsy reports to determine the level of consciousness the prisoners had during their executions. Zivot discovered instead that the inmates had suffered a slower death of organ failure and that they were struggling to breathe as their lungs filled with liquid (Caldwell et al., 2020). This was a case of Pulmonary Edema that was attributed to the first injection of sodium thiopental and discovered to have been present in 84% of the autopsies done on inmates executed by lethal injection (Caldwell et al., 2020). Zivot and his colleague Mark Edgar brought their discoveries to the attention of federal courts in Georgia, Arkansas, Missouri, Tennessee and Ohio, their findings even reached the supreme courts leading to the current controversy and challenges lethal injection as an execution method continues to face (Caldwell et al., 2020).

Gas Chamber

Gas chambers as a form of execution came into existence in the modern era through the story of a prisoner in 1921 from Nevada, U.S.A. (Reggio, n.d., Denno, 2019). Gee Jon was the name of this prisoner, he was a member of the Tong War gang and was convicted of murder for the killing of a rival gang member (Reggio, n.d.). Gee Jon was given a death sentence and the first attempt at the execution method using lethal gas was born when the state executioners tried to pump cyanide gas into his cell at night secretly (Reggio, n.d). According to Reggio (n.d), the state believed this was a humane method of enforcing the penalty because Gee Jon would have been asleep during the attempt, however it was unsuccessful due to technical difficulties. This occasion is what led to the creation of the gas chamber, to carry out the punishment safely, effectively and as humanely as possible (Reggio, n.d). According to California's procedure in carrying out the lethal gas execution method, it takes place in a sealed, modified, octagonal chamber (Denno, 2019). The prisoner is strapped, similarly to the procedure for electric chairs, to a chair that has holes in the seat (Denno, 2019). Underneath the chair, a container of sulfuric acid, distilled water, and sodium cyanide crystals has been placed (Denno, 2019). Denno (2019), states that to activate the gas with those ingredients, the executioner pulls a lever that displaces the cyanide crystals into the container of sulfuric acid-water, this then creates the toxic hydrocyanic gas that kills the prisoner.

What hydrocyanic gas does, is that it destroys a person's ability to process blood hemoglobin leading to death once inhaled (History.com Editors, n.d.). Based on observations of this execution method, some people claim that prisoners fall unconscious within seconds and choke to death but it is hard to determine when they die or measure their pain and consciousness level (Denno, 2019, History.com Editors, n.d). While a lower court strongly believes that the prisoners under the lethal gas suffer a lot of pain that might have lasted minutes and in addition to that some prisoners hold their breath causing them violent convulsions before death (Denno, 2019, History.com Editors, n.d). These beliefs led to a federal appeals court declaring that authorization of lethal gas in California's statute was in violation of U.S. Constitution's Eighth Amendment prohibition against cruel and unusual punishments in 1996 (Denno, 2019), In fact apart from the United States, there has been no other country that has picked up the lethal gas execution method as a way of enforcing their capital punishments (Denno, 2019).

Conclusion

Society has come a long way since the centuries B.C and even the middle ages when it comes to execution methods enforced by empires or the state according to their laws for capital punishment. While death penalty laws have yet to be completely abolished in modern society, concessions and adaptations have been made to accommodate the more civilized culture we live in. Execution methods have been modified with the intent of making it more humane and less cruel to those handed death sentences because today's society does not believe in making them suffer unnecessary pain as punishment. Older methods bordered on being more torturous when executing the accused, and even humiliating them with public executions that made spectacles of their deaths. That has changed and the purpose of this chapter was to show how society and the world in general has evolved in time through their methods of execution.

References

Abbott, G. (2015, May 22). beheading. Encyclopedia Britannica.

Abbott, G. (2007, August 9). boiling. Encyclopedia Britannica.

Alchin, L. (2017). *Burned at the Stake*. Lords and Ladies.

Amnesty International. (n.d.). *Death Penalty in Canada*.

Beccia, C. (2021). *What Happens in a Typical Stoning?* An Injustice Mag.

Bohm, M. R. (2007). *DeathQuest 3: An Introduction to the Theory and Practice of Capital Punishment in the United States* (3rd ed.). Anderson.

Britannica, T. Editors of Encyclopedia (2020, December 23). *hanging. Encyclopedia Britannica.*

Caldwell, L., Chang, A., & Myers, J. (2020). *Gasping For Air: Autopsies Reveal Troubling Effects Of Lethal Injection*. NPR. h

Christopher, I. (2020). *The Plant That Killed Socrates*. Medium.

Crime Museum. (n.d.). *Hanging*.

Crime Museum. (n.d.). *Origins of Capital Punishment*.

Death Penalty Information Center. (n.d.). *Early History of the Death Penalty*.

Death Penalty Information Center. (n.d.). *Description of Each Execution Method*.

Denno, D. W. (2012, February 9). electrocution. Encyclopedia Britannica.

Denno, D. W. (2019, October 21). gas chamber. Encyclopedia Britannica.

Denno, D. W. (2013, September 11). lethal injection. Encyclopedia Britannica.

Egmond, F. (1995). The Cock, the Dog, the Serpent, and the Monkey. Reception and Transmission of a Roman Punishment, or Historiography as History. *International Journal of the Classical Tradition, 2*(2), 159–192.

FindLaw. (2019). *History of Death Penalty Laws*.

Haughton, S. (1866). *On hanging : Considered from a Mechanical and Physiological Point of View*. (pg. 8). The Royal College of Surgeons of England.

History.com Editors. (2020). *First execution by lethal gas*. A & E Television Networks.

Islam, H. P., & Mahabarata, Y. (2020). *When Socrates Was Forced To Commit Suicide Because Of Differences In Views*. VOI.

Layton, J. & Hoyt, A. (2021). *How Does Death by Hanging Work?* HowStuffWorks.

M.ADMIN. (n.d.). *The Weird Roman Punishment That Involved A Sack Full Of Animals.*

Margaritoff, M. (2020). *10 Medieval Execution Methods That Are The Definition Of Cruel And Unusual.* All That's Interesting.

McCombs, B. (2015). *Utah's firing squad: How does it work?* AP News.

fMerriam-Webster. (n.d.). Suicide. *In Merriam-Webster.com dictionary.*

Mukunth, M. (2020). *Gruesome, Clumsy and Irreversible: The Science Behind 'Hanging By the Neck'.* Science the Wire.

NBC News. (2010). *Where is stoning legal, and how is it done?*

New World Encyclopedia. (n.d.). Beheading.

Reinhard, J. R. (1941). Burning at the Stake in Medieval Law and Literature. *Speculum, 16*(2), 186–209.

Reggio, H. M., (n.d.). *History of the Death Penalty.* PBS Frontline.

Retief, F. P., & Cilliers, L. (2003). The history and pathology of crucifixion. *South African medical journal = Suid-Afrikaanse tydskrif vir geneeskunde, 93*(12), 938–941.

Ruth, C. (1984). Sentence of Death by Burning for Women. *The Journal of Legal History, 5*(1), 44-59,

Saunders, M. (2019). *The Torah.* British Library.

5

Who is Eligible for the Death Penalty?

By Alexa Gee

This chapter will discuss the history of the death penalty, showing examples of its use in different parts of the world, throughout many different eras. This chapter will also touch on the various methods of execution used. Then, it will highlight the rules of eligibility and ineligibility for the death penalty, with a focus on the American and Canadian penal system and their laws. Finally, this chapter will discuss which demographics are most likely to be given the death penalty, with a focus on the United States.

History of the Death Penalty

The origins of the death penalty can be traced as far back as the 18th century BC in the kingdom of Babylon (Death Penalty Information Center. Records known as the Code of King Hammurabi stated the death penalty could be used for 25 different crimes. The death penalty has also been seen as a sentence found in the 14th century BC Hittite Code, the 7th century BC Draconian Code of Athens for all crimes, and the 5th century BC Roman Law of 12 Tablets. Sentences could be carried out through crucifixion, drowning, beating to death, burned alive, or impaled (Death Penalty Information Center, n.d.).

By the 10th century AD, in Britain, hanging was the most used method of execution (Death Penalty Information Center, n.d.). This changed in the next century when William the Conqueror only allowed hanging for times of war. In the time of King Henry VIII, around 72 000 people were executed by beheading, boiling, drawing and quartering, or other methods not limited to times of war. Executions could be treason, marrying a Jewish person, among many other offences. By the 1700s, jurors had discretion not to impose the death penalty for lesser crimes, such as stealing (Death Penalty Information Center, n.d.). Starting in 1823, reforms were made to cut the number of punishable crimes by the death penalty from 222 crimes to around 100 eligible crimes.

The British system has influenced former colonies like Canada and US's parameters for the death penalty (Death Penalty Information Center, n.d.). Starting from early American colonial history to the present day, 464 Native Americans have legally been executed, although this number does not account for the other extra-judicial genocide of many other Indigenous peoples (Death Penalty Information Center, n.d.). In the United States, the most common reason those convicted of a crime is given the death penalty for a murder charge (Death Penalty Information Center, n.d.). Other crimes involving the death of the victims are also reasons for death penalty eligibility.

Other capital offences including treason, kidnapping, drug trafficking, bombing, and espionage may result in the death penalty (Death Penalty Information Center, n.d.). Some states have previously allowed for a death penalty sentence for the rape of a child, like the state of Texas, Louisiana, Georgia, Montana, and South Carolina. This sentence was most often used against black men for their crimes against white women. It was ruled by the Supreme Court that this was a cruel and unusual punishment, so these offenders are no longer eligible for the death penalty. See below for more eligibility rules.

Abolishment of the Death Penalty

United States
About half the states in the United States have not abolished the death penalty as of 2022 (World Population Review, 2020). The death penalty is still in place for those in Montana, Idaho, Oklahoma, Texas, Arizona, Tennessee, Georgia, Florida, South Dakota, Wyoming, Utah, Nevada, Louisiana, Alabama, Ohio, Indiana, Mississippi, Arkansas, Kentucky, Nebraska, Missouri, North Carolina, South Carolina, and Kansas. Texas has had the most executions since 1976.

Internationally, as of 2019, 142 countries have abolished the death penalty, with only 56 countries still using it as a sentence (European Parliament, 2020). Many European countries stopped executions in the early to late 20th century. Portugal had the last date of execution in 1849 and many other Western European countries abolished the death penalty completely in the 1970s. The United Kingdom abolished the death penalty in the same year as Canada.

Canada
In Canada, the last execution happened in 1962, in Toronto where Ronald Turpin and Arthur Lucas were killed by hanging (Amnesty International, 2022). It is signed into law so there can be no return to the death penalty in Canada. This means that there is no offence in Canada eligible for the death penalty. Before Canada became a country, many criminal offences were punishable by death, ac-

cording to British law (Gendreau & Renke, 2006). In 1749, in the newly established Halifax, Peter Carcel, was charged and executed for murder. In 1865, murder, treason, and rape were considered the only capital offences. In total, 710 prisoners have been executed in Canada. After 1976, those who were members of the Armed Forces could be executed if they were found guilty of cowardice, desertion, unlawful surrender, or spying for the enemy. The last people to be executed in Canada are Arthur Lucas and Ronald Turpin, in 1962 (Alamenciak, 2012). In 1998, the death penalty was officially abolished in Canada.

Other Death Penalties: Asia

While many countries around the world have now abolished the death penalty, the majority of countries in the continent of Asia still have some form of capital punishment (Death Penalty Information Center, n.d.). Below is a discussion of some of these countries that still have the death penalty.

Singapore

Singapore has one of the harshest death penalties in the world (Ministry of Home Affairs, 2021). Relative to its population size, it has one of the highest execution rates, including the executions of foreign nationals. The exact number of those currently subjected to execution is unknown, as the use of the death penalty is shrouded from international viewers (Amnesty International, n.d.). The death penalty is in place as a deterrence for other similar future crimes, although this fact is debated (Ministry of Home Affairs, 2021; Amnesty International, n.d.). In a study comparing the murder rates of Singapore and a city of similar population size, Hong Kong, where the death penalty was abolished in 1993 (Yap, 2022). It was found that the murder rate was not influenced by the death penalty (Cribb, 2004). Murder, trafficking of drugs, or the illegal use of firearms are some of the offences eligible for the penalty, depending on the level of harm done to the victim and society (Ministry of Home Affairs, 2021). Many death penalty sentences are for drug trafficking, where the movement of drugs above a certain weight carries mandatory death sentences (Amnesty International, n.d.).

This law created great controversy when a Malaysian citizen, considered mentally disabled, was executed for a drug offence in 2022 (Ng & Soo, 2022). Nagaenthran Dharmalingam was caught trafficking 43 grams of heroin into Singapore. The execution of a mentally ill person is prohibited under international human rights law, though Singapore courts ruled that despite proof of mental illness, Dharmalingam understood the actions of his crime. Anyone who attempts to cross the border into Singapore with over 15 grams of heroin faces the death sentence, as the laws are made clear at the border, according to Singapore's government (Ng & Soo, 2022). The Malaysian government had called out Singapore's treatment of Dharmalingam, although their laws surrounding the death penalty are strict as well.

Malaysia

Malaysia also has strict punishments for drugs; two-thirds of people on death row are for drug offences (Lakhdir, 2022). Up until the 1990s, Malaysia's sentencing for drug crimes was considered the harshest in the world (Amnesty International, n.d.). 73% of all prisoners on death row were drug trafficking. In what some call a similar case to the highly controversial sentence of Dharmalingam in Singapore, they executed a convicted man for trafficking 2.3 kg of methamphetamine (Lakhdir, 2022). Aside from drug trafficking, murder, treason, terrorism, and waging war against the ruler of Malaysia are among the other crimes punishable by the death penalty (Amnesty International, n.d.) Judges do have some discretion when sentencing, but this has led to accusations of the arbitrary nature of giving the death sentence (Yap, 2022).

Indonesia

Like Malaysia and Singapore, many prisoners on death row in Indonesia are for drug offences (Lubis, 2015). Indonesia has introduced a new rule in its draft of an updated Criminal Code, where if the death row convict shows the ability to rehabilitate for their crime, the sentence can be reduced to life in prison or 20 years in prison (Lubis, 2015).

Eligibility

Capital Crimes

A capital offence is a crime that is punishable by the death penalty (Savitz, 1955). Murder, treason, bombings, and other serious offences have or are considered capital offences, depending on the jurisdiction. After Coker v. Georgia, 1977, the US Supreme Court ruled that the penalty for a crime must be proportional to the crime by the 8th amendment, which bars cruel and unusual punishments (Cornell Law School, n.d.). There are three factors to consider when sentencing: the gravity of the offence, the stringency of the penalty, and how the jurisdiction punishes other criminals for the same crime. The death penalty for child rape, allowed in six states, Louisiana, Montana, Georgia, Oklahoma, South Carolin, and Texas, was considered disproportionate in 2008.

When giving the death sentence, a judge, along with a jury, must be present. There is a two-stage trial, to determine innocence or guilt, considering any aggravating or mitigating circumstances when sentencing (ACLU, n.d.). There are five methods allowed: hanging in Delaware, New Hampshire, and Washington, firing squad only in Idaho and Utah, electrocution, gas chamber, or lethal injection. Electrocution was most widely used until the use of lethal injection in Texas in 1982. As of 2022, there have only been two people on death row for a non-murder charge, Patrick Kennedy and Richard Davis, in Louisiana (Death Penalty Information Center, n.d.).

Foreign Nationals

Those who are citizens of other countries can be tried in the United States and given the death penalty (Death Penalty Information Center, n.d.). Many other countries have tried foreign nationals on their soil, like Singapore and Malaysia (Amnesty International, n.d.). Their treatment is under the Vienna Convention on Consular Relations treaty, which governs the treatment of one nation's citizens when arrested in a different country. However, the United States Supreme Court has been accused of violating this treaty several times; the Supreme Court has said that requiring states to comply with the treaty requires an act of congress.

Ineligibility

Mental Disability

Those ineligible for the death penalty are those with mental handicaps since this is considered a violation of the eighth amendment and this lessens the severity of the crime, as determined by Atkins v. Virginia in 2002 (Cornell Law School, n.d.). Hall v. Florida determined that a low IQ threshold cannot determine whether someone is intellectually disabled (Cornell Law School, n.d.).

Juveniles

The eligibility of the death penalty for juveniles has changed throughout the history of the United States (Savitz, 1955). In the colony of Plymouth, Massachusetts in 1642, Thomas Graunger, was the first juvenile executed in American history. In total, 226 juveniles have been given the death penalty since 1973; at the time of execution, all the offenders were over the age of 18.

Juveniles were eligible for the death penalty until the Roper v. Simmons case in 2005, which ruled that those under 18 could not be sentenced to death because of the lack of maturity, vulnerability to negative influences, and lack of mental development (ACLU, n.d.;

Cornell Law School, n.d.). Previously, in Thompson v. Oklahoma (1988), the Supreme Court prohibited the execution of those 15 or younger due to the death sentence being a cruel or unusual punishment (Death Penalty Information Center, n.d.). However, 19 states still permitted the execution of those who are 16-17 years of age, through the ruling of the Supreme Court cases of Wilkins v. Missouri and Stanford v. Kentucky in 1989. Now, juveniles are ineligible for the death penalty since 2005; those who were on death row had their sentences changed to life in prison.

Aside from the United States, the countries Iran, Pakistan, China, South Sudan, the Democratic Republic of Congo, Nigeria, Yemen, and Saudi Arabia have also executed juveniles, though these cases are not frequent (Amnesty International, 2019). Since 2009, only Iran, Saudi Arabia, and Sudan have executed offenders who were still juveniles at the time of the execution, with Iran having executed the most.

Who is Most Likely to get the Death Penalty?

Racial Bias
In the United States, there is strong discrimination in the death row population based on race, geography, socioeconomic status, and gender. Racial bias is rampant in the southern states, where black men are more likely to be given the death penalty than a white offender if they murder or rape a white person (ACLU, n.d.).

Over 3200 men are under the death sentence in the US (Death Penalty Information Center, n.d.). As of January 2022, there are 692 death row prisoners total who are awaiting execution in California, the highest population; Florida follows that number with 330 prisoners on death row. The race of the defendant and/ or the race of the victim is a strong factor in many of the states with the death penalty. Only a handful convicted of murdering a person of colour has gotten the death sentence (Death Penalty Information Center, n.d.). Texas, Louisiana, California, Nebraska, and Mississippi all have greater than 60% of people of colour on death row, with Texas having the highest number at 73.4 % (Death Penalty Information Center, 2022). In Washington State, black defendants are three times more likely to be recommended for the death sentence than a white defendant of an equivalent case is. Black people have a 3.5% higher chance of getting the death penalty if the victim was white. Cases involving white victims are 97% more likely to receive death sentences than black victims in Louisiana. The victims of those on death row are 75% white even though only 50% of murder victims are white.

The incarceration rate of Indigenous peoples is 38% higher than the national average in the United States (Death Penalty Information Center, n.d.). There are several cases where Native Americans have been given the death penalty unjustly. For example, the Supreme Court rules that Oklahoma lacked jurisdiction to prosecute Indigenous nations part of the Muscogee Reservation since Congress never disestablished this reservation.

Other than the United States, racial bias is prevalent in many other countries. In Malaysia, the Indian population is overrepresented in the total death row population, while Malaysians are overrepresented (Yap, 2022). In Canada, the Supreme Court of Canada, in R v. Williams, ruled that systemic racism contributed to the disproportionate representation of Indigenous people in the penal system. This traces back to the early years of Canada's official recognition as a country, such as the famous hanging of Louis Riel for his action in the North-West Rebellion (Law Explorer, 2015).

Gender Bias

Women account for only 2% of those on death row, which is disproportionately less than the 11% of women who make up criminal homicides (ACLU, n.d.). Women who have killed men, typically after being abused by these men, are more likely to get the death penalty than a female victim. Only 51 women have been executed, one woman since 1975, with a bias toward black women (15/51).

Socioeconomic status

Those who could not afford a lawyer are more likely to end up on death row, so the population of offenders waiting to be executed is made up of those with low socioeconomic status (ACLU, n.d.). This was found to be true in other countries, such as Malaysia, especially among those who are not educated in the Bahasa Malaysia language (Yap, 2022).

Execution of the Innocent

There are several cases where an innocent person has been handed the death sentence, for a variety of reasons (Death Penalty Information Center, n.d.). When giving the death penalty, the jury may not always comprehend the laws or be swayed to believe the accused is guilty. In some cases, those who are innocent have been given the death penalty and unjustly executed. The death penalty is typically irreversible unless the court is willing to listen to new evidence showing proof of innocence at an impossibly high standard. Racial bias, inadequate police work, coerced confessions, prior records, under-resourced defense, community pressure, and other factors result in an unjust system toward the innocent. Some are advised to plead guilty to a crime they did not commit because they plead innocent and are found guilty they are more likely to get the death penalty. Recent cases, like Troy Davis who was a black man executed for murdering a white police officer, were a miscarriage of justice (Selby, n.d.). There are many similar cases of black men on death row for crimes they did not commit in the United States. On average, 3.94 wrongfully convicted death row prisoners have been exonerated every year since 1973, although many more innocents have been executed (Death Penalty Information Center, n.d.). The chapter, "Stay of Execution" will expand on this topic.

Conclusion

This chapter gave an overview of the various places in which the death penalty is legal, or was previously legal. The death penalty has a long history of use, going back to ancient times. It is still in practice today, many offenders in Asian countries, the United States, and many other jurisdictions await execution. Eligibility rules for the death penalty have changed in light of Supreme Court rulings on fairness and justice. There is bias when giving the death penalty. Those of low socioeconomic status, from a marginalized background, or who identify as men are more likely to be given the death sentence.

References

ACLU. (n.d.). *Death penalty 101*. American Civil Liberties Union.

ACLU. (n.d.). *Juveniles and the death penalty*. American Civil Liberties Union.

ACLU. (n.d.). *The case against the death penalty*. American Civil Liberties Union.

Alamenciak, T. (2012, December 10). *The end of the rope: The story of Canada's last executions*.

Amnesty International. (n.d.). *Death penalty in Canada*. Amnesty International Canada.

Amnesty International . (2020, January 7). *A brief history of the death penalty in Malaysia*. Amnesty International Malaysia.

Amnesty International . (2021, February 2). *Abolish death penalty*. Amnesty International Malaysia.

Cornell Law School. (n.d.). *Death penalty*. Legal Information Institute.

Cribb, T. (2004, March 22). *Demise of the death penalty*. South China Morning Post.

David, D. (2022, April 27). *Kuching High Court sentences man to death for trafficking 2.3kg of meth*. Borneo Post Online.

Death Penalty Information Center . (n.d.). *Death Penalty Information Center Fact Sheet*. Death Penalty Information Center .

Death Penalty Information Center. (n.d.). *Early history of the death penalty*. Death Penalty Information Center.

Death Penalty Information Center. (n.d.). *Executions around the world*. Death Penalty Information Center.

Death Penalty Information Center. (n.d.). *Executions of juveniles outside of the U.S.* Death Penalty Information Center.

Death Penalty Information Center. (n.d.). *Native Americans*. Death Penalty Information Center.

Death Penalty Information Center. (n.d.). *Foreign nationals*. Death Penalty Information Center.

Death Penalty Information Center. (n.d.). *The juvenile death penalty prior to Roper v. Simmons*. Death Penalty Information Center.

Death Penalty Information Center. (n.d.). *Winter 2022 death row USA: State death rows drop below 2,400 for first time since 1990*. Death Penalty Information Center.

European Parliament. (2020, July 28). *Death penalty in Europe and the rest of the world: Key facts: News: European parliament*. Death penalty in Europe and the rest of the world: key facts | News | European Parliament. R

Gendreau, P., & Renke, W. (2006). *Capital punishment in Canada*. The Canadian Encyclopedia.

Lakhdhir, L. (2022, April 28). *Malaysia's death penalty hypocrisy*. Human Rights Watch.

Law Explorer. (n.d.). *The death penalty in Canada: Ethnicity, abolition and the current debate*. Law Explorer.

Ng, E., & Soo, Z. (2022, April 27). *Singapore executes mentally disabled man, ignoring pleas*. Time.

Savitz, L. D. (1955). Capital Crimes as defined in American statutory law. *The Journal of Criminal Law, Criminology, and Police Science, 46*(3), 355.

Selby, D. (2020, September 22). *Nine years after the execution of Troy Davis, innocent black men are still being sentenced to death*. Innocence Project.

Singapore Government . (2021). *The Death Penalty in Singapore*. Ministry of Home Affairs.

Yap, B. (2022, March 4). *Malaysia should scrap the death penalty once and for all. – The Diplomat*.

World Population Review . (2022). Death penalty states 2022.

6

Psychological Impacts Behind the Death Penalty

by Karen Therese Pangan

✢

A comprehensive understanding of the psychological impacts of the death penalty requires taking the perspectives of the variety of demographics involved. While there are other bodies that may be affected by the broader concept of capital punishment, including researchers and political advocates for or against the penalty, there are three main bodies that are directly affected by a single individual's death sentencing. The first to be considered are the inmates themselves, who ironically live with their sentence for years prior to their execution date in conditions worse than the general prison population, with many continuously appealing to the state to avoid death. Legal bodies and executioners who manage the lives of these inmates are also profoundly affected by the gravity of their work, with the former being under the pressure of protecting a life from death while simultaneously understanding the breadth of their client's wrongdoings, and the latter being the party involved in the inmate's final moments. Finally, the grief and at times motivating rage felt by the families of both the inmate as well as their victims is complicated and possibly contradictory to one's own moral compass, as it is coupled with the factors of understanding the evidence against their loved one and the gravity of the inmates' punishment itself. Though limited in the research by access of records to mainly American history and methodology, this chapter will examine the environments and testimonies of those impacted in the death processes to support psychological phenomena and the implications of such on the death penalty process and the legitimacy of state violence as a whole.

Part I: Death Row Inmates

The Final Years

A defiant stare, a broken nib, and the camera cuts to shots of an individual dying by sedative, electric chair, or feet dangling from a noose. While popular media varies in the portrayal of the process of being on death row, it is often implicated that the decision to sentence someone to death and the process of taking their life is a quick decision. This may have a hint of accuracy in historical death penalties such as torturous executions of the Salem witch trials and the lynchings in the pre-Civil War Era, but the current reality of the death penalty in American culture is not at all immediate. Despite slight variations with averages (coming from the consideration of previous incarceration time irrelevant to an individuals' death sentence), with the Death Penalty Information Center (DPIC) stating an average of 20.25 years of living on death row as of 2017 (DPIC, 2022) and the Bureau of Justice reporting an average of 18.7 years of living on death row as of 2021 (Snell, 2021), the range between these two figures emphasizes the great length of time a death row inmate spends prior to death. From a logical and ethical perspective, this great length of time leads to a higher understanding of an inmate's case and the full extent of who was involved in the crime and who was victimized. Time is necessary in ensuring that the right person is brought to justice for the right reasons. However, in this time an individual is also incarcerated regardless of their innocence, and nearly two decades of their lifetime is consumed. In these two decades, the death row inmate experiences a unique environment, with limited social interactions and limited social support. The result of this unique environment has been studied in further detail in recent decades, with an increased dedication of research leading to the discovery of mental health problems unique to the death row context, namely death row phenomenon and death row syndrome.

The analysis of the social interactions between death row inmates and certain populations reveals a master status that comes with being a death row inmate. Regardless of who interacts with them, the demographics that directly interact with death row inmates treat them as an entity close to human, but not quite. In one compilation of the accounts of Ohio Death Row inmates, Eric Lose describes death row inmates in the Mansfield Correctional Institute (ManCI) as "respected and feared" (Lose, 2014, p. 19) by other medium security inmates, and even a mere wave from a death row inmate changes the behaviours of prisoners to "subservient fashion" (Lose, 2014, p. 20). The prisoners' combined reaction of fear and respect towards death row inmates is akin to how one might react to a ghost. Later in the same chapter Lose explains how social interactions with outsiders require two things: first, outsiders wishing to visit must go through a complicated process of x-ray scanners, multiple institutional gates, and winding hall-ways (Lose, 2014, pp 20-23) that death row inmates be physically chained and bound, for example with "bracelets...attached to a 4-foot chain that would encircle [the death row inmate's] waist... padlocked in the back" (Lose, 2014, 24). Lose's account indicates the treatment of death row inmates as a dangerous, wild animal. Despite the detail Lose provides in his book, these two conditions seem to be the only source of the limited social interactions for death row inmates. According to the Death Penalty Information

Center, death row inmates "are generally isolated from other prisoners...and sharply restricted in terms of visitation and exercise, spending as many as 23 hours a day alone in their cells" (DPIC, 2019). In debates against the death penalty this isolation is often scrutinized, with many critics of the death penalty arguing that the near complete isolation for a prolonged period of time is inhumane and leads to psychological problems for the inmates. Indeed, this isolation condition in conjunction with the increasing stress of appealing their death sentence has resulted in a variety of mental health problems for death row inmates, namely the death row phenomenon and death row syndrome.

In 1989, Jens Soering awaited the ruling that would determine whether or not he would be sent to Virginia's Death Row in the United States of America. After murdering William Reginald Haysom and Nancy Astor Haysom in Bedford County, Virginia, Soering as well as his then-girlfriend and accomplice, Elizabeth Haysom, confessed their crimes to United Kingdom police and investigators a year after fleeing the country (Icelandic Human Rights Centre [IHRC], [n. d.]). The gravity of his crime coupled with the evidence against him lead Virginia authorities to seek the death penalty for Soering. In the Soering v. The United Kingdom Case, Soering's team makes the argument against his surrender to the United States on the grounds that he "[dreaded] extreme physical violence and homosexual abuse from other inmates in death row in Virginia...[this had] a profound psychological effect on him... that he may seek to take his own life." (Icelandic Human Rights Centre [IHRC], [n. d.]). This is one of the first documented mentions of the death row phenomenon in an applied legal case (DPIC, 2022), where it was argued as a form of "torture [or] inhuman or degrading treatment or punishment" (IHRC, [n. d.]). Death row phenomenon is a topic of increasing research in the debate against death penalty, and is "used to describe the harmful effects of death row conditions, including exposure to extended periods of solitary confinement and the mental anxiety that prisoners experience while waiting for their death" (Harrison & Tamony, 2010). While this specific phrase is used to describe Soering's mental state, a more acute labelling of his distress and suicidal thinking can be found with death row syndrome, which describes the "consequential psychological illness that can occur as a result of death row phenomenon" (Harrison & Tamony, 2010). The relationship between these two terms is similar to the difference between feeling anxiety (or feeling the effects of the death row phenomenon) vs. being diagnosed with general anxiety disorder (being diagnosed with a mental illness and qualifying for death row syndrome), with the differentiating factor being the diagnosis of mental illness(es). Therefore, Soering's status as a 'suicide-risk prisoner' qualifies his death row syndrome. Though their legitimacy is still being debated and neither is recognized in western diagnostic tools for mental illnesses such as the *Diagnostic and Statistical Manual of Mental Disorders* (DSM-5) or the *International Classification of Diseases* (ICD-11), the surface-level definition of death row syndrome as the onset of mental illnesses is supported in recent studies of mental health issues in death row inmates, such as depression (Harave et al., 2021).

Despite the increasing recognition of mental illness problems such as death row phenomenon and death row syndrome, there is limited support in death row. Not only for psychological well-being but also for educational and employment opportunities during their stay in death row. American death row inmates currently have access to psychiatric help, as American law indicates that every person "have the right to physical and mental health treatment up until the very moment that they are executed" (Yanofski, 2011). The decision of whether mental health professionals should be participating in death penalty processing is controversial, as some argue that their testimony of the inmate has the possibility to violate their Hippocratic Oath, by being damning, harming evidence against their client (Kermani & Drob, 1988). Regardless of this debate, it is undeniable that psychiatrists have a vital role, not only in the assessment of a death row inmate's mental well-being, but also as another source in testimony and the legal processes. At times, their testimony can also help inmates avoid the death penalty in the first place. This pattern is evident in the earlier case of Soering, notably how Dr. Somekh's testimony had been a decisive factor in determining Soering's distress and mental state. However, even if mental health support did work in favor of the death row inmates, their overall social support remains limited, as they are "excluded from prison educational and employment programs" (DPIC, 2022, para. 5). In the event that death row inmates appeal their death sentence and are exonerated, their decades spend in isolation with limited social support will no doubt follow them for the rest of their lives, affecting their overall functioning.

The Final Moments

While the psychological states of a death row inmate's final moments are more difficult to decipher, some studies have implicated insight on the mental states of death row inmates through processes such as last meal choices. In a study regarding the guilt levels of death row inmates and the nutritional data of their last meats, Cornell researchers Kevin M. Kniffin and Brian Wansink found that death row inmates in the United States of America who "[admitted] guilt are relatively more 'at peace' with their sentence" (Kniffin & Wansick, 2013, p.1) and request more food. The concept of having found peace in these last moments follows societal expectations of hardened criminals, but this may have a sinister implication. This moment of peace can also be interpreted as the same core characteristic in antisocial personality disorder and psychopathy: lack of reaction in the face of threatening situations. While not yet proven empirically, this is important to consider, especially with the high correlation between antisocial personality disorder and criminal activity (Fridell et al., 2008).

Part II: Legal Representatives and Executioners

Perhaps the most indirect of the three demographics discussed in this chapter would be legal representatives and the executioners of the death penalty itself, with the overarching pressure of being involved in the choice of life or death for the accused. For the first demographic of legal representatives for the death row inmate, their psychological effects can be tied to the pressures of advocating for their client in hopes of sparing their life. Executioners have a different pressure, instead with the direct involvement of taking a life on behalf of the state.

Legal Representatives

Because of attorney-client privileges, not much is known about the specific interactions between lawyers and their death row clients, but researchers have gleaned broad patterns in the philosophies and psychologies of death row lawyers. Though they have a comprehensive understanding of the extent of their client's crime and guilt, writer David G. Scout (1988) writes that death row lawyers continue to advocate for the accused based on their belief that "killing murderers is wrong" (p. 2), despite what outside opinions may feel. However, this guiding philosophy comes at a cost to the lawyer. From the economic perspective, the hefty expense of death penalty legal costs does include lawyers for the death row inmate (DPIC, 2021, para. 5). However, because of the lack of capital defense organizations, representation for the United States have limited budgets (DPIC, 2021, para. 3), and Scout notes that lawyers work "long hours for low pay" (Scout, 1988, p.3). This same working pattern reflects in the psychological states of lawyers, who therefore experience acute stress (Penal Reform International [PRI], 2014, p. 1). Penal Reform International (2014) directly quotes a number of emotional states, such as "numbness, sadness, anger, panic reactions, flashbacks, and feelings of dissociation or depression that can last for days, weeks, even months or years" (p. 2). Not only is this stress influenced by economic factors, but it is also influenced by emotional factors. In their pursuit of defending death row inmates, lawyers are also acutely aware of the social inequalities in the country that they believe have led to their client's incarceration, and the personal motivation of having "a life in [the lawyers'] hands" (PRI, 2014, p.1). In one account, a lawyer has described this stress as "paralyzing, feeling like you're going to come out of your skin, feeling like you're losing it, or screaming." (PRI, 2014, p.1). Despite this immense impact, Penal Reform International argues that lawyers are often unprepared for the scope of the emotional impact of work in capital punishment, and are often unable to talk about their emotions due to lack of professional training and social norms within their line of work.

Executioners

Executioners face the same nuances as lawyers do, with the difference of having direct contact with the death row inmate at their death. Many deciding factors influence the range of emotion and opinion executioners have regarding the death penalty and their profession, from their opinions of the justice system to personal philosophies. As well, there is a range of execution methods that vary in time and state, but regardless of how physically close they are to the inmate, going through with the act of execution does affect the mental well-being of these state workers. In an account from Jerry Givens to The Guardian, he states a feeling of deep regret in accepting the job as an executioner. The prison-guard-turned-executioner states that "if [he] had known what [he] had to go through as an executioner, [he] wouldn't have done it." (Givens, 2013, question 5). In the interview he acknowledges the impact of his work, and discusses the realities of the justice system in Virginia, U.S.A., and his consistent efforts in awareness of the details of death row. He achieves this level of social action by speaking with school children, writing his book, Another Day Not Promised and is active in his community, working as one of the administrative staff on Virginians for Alternatives to the Death Penalty after his leave from the position of the state's executioner. Even while separated from the direct involvement of the death penalty, Givens continues to participate in the debate behind its morality, on the basis of unfair trial practices and the inequality of the American justice system.

Part III: Victims and Relations to Death Row Inmates

Beyond the initial criminal act of the death row inmate, two types of families remain impacted psychologically, as indirect victims to the inmate's sentencing to capital punishment. The first type includes families and close relations to the victims of the death row inmates, either by their death or through another form of tragedy. This demographic is unique as their trauma combines the grief of losing their loved one or having them affected by the criminal's actions, as well as their own ethical standards in the pursuit of their justice. The second type of family are ones close to the inmate that is on death row. They also have a complicated relationship with grief, combining the loss of their loved one with the understanding of what they have done. While the ambiguity between these two types of grief held by these families is one of their similarities, they also have their differences in their nuances.

Families of the Victims

In seeking justice in the face of tragedy, families of victims are exposed to and often look into the eyes of the people responsible for harming their loved one. In cases of homicides of a magnitude grand enough for juries to consider capital punishment, the pain and media attention inflicted by the death row inmate and their case create lasting impacts on the lives of the victims and their families. This trauma becomes more complicated as victims advocate in court for justice, by wanting the very thing that took away their loved one: the death of the murderer.

Despite the differences in grief patterns in homicide victim's families, researchers of this explore similar themes as Kubler-Ross' five stages model of denial and isolation, anger, bargaining, depression, and acceptance (Kubler-Ross, 1969). For example, the National Organization of Victim Assistance (NOVA) considers the stages survivors of homicide victims go through as denial, protest/anger, despair, detachment, and deconstruction of life (Vollum, 2008, p.12).

In many cases of the murder victim's families, their encompassing rage and grief may motivate them to push for capital punishment towards their loved one's killer as justice and revenge. In Scott Vollum's work Last Words and the Death Penalty: Voices of the Condemned and Their Co-Victims, he notes the work of other researchers, with one applicable grief pattern to the demographic in question. He argues that the "fear and vulnerability" caused by the grief of losing one's loved one to homicide can be "accompanied by desires for revenge or retaliation, as explored by Greg Mitchell, Robert Jay Lifton, and Austin Sarat (Vollum, 2008, p. 12). This is also supported by Kenneth J. Doka's work, as he states that this demographic's "normal anger associated with grief is compounded by the rage and desire to destroy the murderer of the loved one" (Doka, 1996, p.53).

In Families of Homicide Victims Speak: An Examination of Perceptions of the Criminal System and Capital Punishment, Dr. Jamie Lynn Burns finds the common motive of closure from the victim's families choosing to witness the execution of the death row inmate responsible for causing harm to their loved ones. She quotes a particular responded as "[doing] something in honor of them (their loved one)" (Burns, 2006, p. 112), and states other reasons for witnessing the execution as "retribution and to see the long process come to an end" (Burns, 2006, p. 111). The sense of honor and closure are the motivating factors in a family's drive to bring justice to their offender, but this is not the only reason why these families would prefer their punishment in the first place. Taking the same context of the United States of America, Dr. Burns notes that in homicide cases reaching the magnitude of considering the death penalty, the jury only has two options in deciding an offender's sentence: "life without parole [or] capital punishment" (Burns, 2006, p. 94). Burns notes that life without parole is too lenient of a sentence for families of the victim as though it does technically indicate life imprisonment, it does not guarantee incarceration for the criminal for the rest of their life, as these families believe that criminal justice system policies do not ensure the offender will never be released. Even when not fueled by revenge and retaliation to the point of death, families of murder victims sometimes have no other choice for justice.

Families of the Inmates

"Did you kill Mr. and Mrs. Sherrill? Did you cause their deaths?" Katherine Norgard waits for her son's response to the prosecutor's question. Moments later, Norgard cringed with her entire body, a response to his chilling "Yes" (King, 2005, p. 282). In months prior to this hearing, Norgard has grappled with the intense commotion surrounding her son, John Eastlack's criminal activity. The discovery of her son's brutal murder of an elderly couple in Tucson has deeply affected her life, from disrupting her work as a university professor and psychotherapist, to her personal relationships with her other child and husband, becoming more absent in her coping with grief. Greatly affected by the process of her son's hearings through hearing his rationalization and admittance to the crime, hearing the state's solution of capital punishment, and how incomprehensible her heartbreak was, Norgard's life shifted, with the goal of saving her son becoming her "primary focus…[being] center stage for [Norgard]" (King, 2005, 289). In her account as presented by Rachel King, Norgard's account provides insight into how families of the condemned explore how the process of bringing justice from a death row criminal fundamentally affects their lives through persisting damage to their reputations and their increased motivation to abolish capital punishment itself.

The particular demographic of families of death row inmates have a complex trauma; their grief of losing a family member mixes with the slow acceptance of the crime they have committed. As with Norgard's case, many families continue to be haunted by the actions of their loved ones, even beyond their initial death sentence. In her case, her employment status became increasingly unstable, as her legitimacy as a psychotherapist and as a graduate professor was called into question, as she states "[needing] to tell each one of [her] psychotherapy clients" (King, 2005, p. 276) to disclose her relationship with her son. Not only would this stigma only affect their employment positions, but can also affect different areas in the family member's social standing. The National Child Traumatic Stress Network notes how children with familial connections to death row inmates may experience "stigma, judgement, and exclusion from natural supports", and "shamed, harassed, or excluded" by members of society with their connection to their family's criminal activity, no matter how directly related or how close of a relationship they had (The National Child Traumatic Stress Network [NCTSN], 2021, p. 3). All of these societal pressures co-occur with the complex grief of losing a member in the first place.

Norgard's personal relationships with her daughter and her husband became rocky in their differing coping mechanisms, and Norgard never being fully present for either of them (King, 2005, p. 289). This reflects another aspect of this family's grief: increased devotion to the accused leading to the deterioration of family dynamics outside of the death row inmate. The grief of losing a family member can lead to a chain reaction in which families lose more than one member from the amount of time that family member gives to the case. Either by testimony, working on their case, or participating in the debate of the death penalty by dedicating time, research, and work. In this case, the coping mechanism Norgard pursued as a result of losing John Eastlack led to further problems in her relationship with her daughter and her husband (King, 2005).

As implied, in some cases this grief pushes them to become louder public critics of capital punishment itself, providing a unique perspective on the harrowing process. Norgard herself becomes an avid writer and critic of the death penalty, becoming an author advocating against it in books such as Hard to Place: A Crime of Alcohol, which explores her relationship with her son, John

Eastlack (Fimbres, 2006, para. 5). She would not be the only case study as a family member resisting capital punishment. The family of Duis Akim became loud critics of the death penalty where in an report by his mother quotes "[feeling] a loss already although the execution has yet to be carried out" (Fong, 2018, para. 12) and that "imprisonment is enough of a sentence for them" (Fong, 2018, para. 13).

Conclusion

The variation in the psychological standing among the demographics of death row inmates, legal representatives, executioners, and the familial relations of both victims and inmates enlightens public opinion of the direct effects of the death penalty. Their testimonies, stories, and research exhibits how capital punishment affects an individual, their relationships, personal philosophy, opinion, and in some cases, further advocacy and participation in the debate of the death penalty itself, and how it psychologically impacts the people who may not be in the electric chair in the first place. Every single account of these people is vital to the debate of capital punishment, providing a foundation in the discussion of its future, its legitimacy, and its role in the pursuit of justice.

References

Burns, J. L. (2006). *Families of homicide victims speak: an examination of perceptions of the criminal justice system and capital punishment.* ProQuestion Information and Learning Company.

Death Penalty Information Center. (2019, August 7). *Conditions on death row.* Death Penalty Information Center.

Death Penalty Information Center. (2021, February 23). *Costs.* Death Penalty Information Center.

Death Penalty Information Center. (2022, April 25). *Time on death row.* Death Penalty Information Center.

Doka, K. J. (Ed.). (1996). *Living with grief after sudden loss: Suicide, homicide, accident, heart attack, stroke.* Hospice Foundation of America.

Fimbres, G. (2006, February 25) *Alcohol: A preventable crime.* Tucson Citizen.

Fong, D. R. (2018, December 26). Families of death row inmates pray for end to death penalty. *Free Malaysia Today.*

Fridell, M., Hesse, M., Jæger, M. M., & Kühlhorn, E. (2018, June). Antisocial personality disorder as a predictor of criminal behaviour in a longitudinal study of a cohort of abusers of several classes of drugs: Relation to type of substance and type of crime. *Addictive Behaviours. 33*(6), 799-811.

Givens, J. (2013, November 21). I was Virginia's executioner from 1982 to 1999: Any questions for me? *The Guardian.*

Harave, V. S., Sastry, N. B., & Devarayadurga, G. V. (2021, May 5). A cross-sectional study of depression among death row convicts from a south indian state. *Kerala Journal of Psychiatry. 34*(1), 35-39.

Harrison, K., & Tamony, A. (2010). Death row phenomenon, death row syndrome and their affect on capital cases in the US. *Internet Journal of Criminology.*

Kermani, E. J., & Drob, S. L. (1988). Psychiatry and the death penalty: Dilemma for mental health professionals. *Psychiatric Quarterly. 59*(3), 193-212.

King, R. (1963). *Capital consequences: Families of the condemned tell their stories.* Rutgers University Press.

Kniffin, K. M., & Wansink, B. (2013, December 20). Death row confessions and the last meal test of innocence. *Laws. 3*, 1-11.

Kübler-Ross, E. (1969). *On death and dying.* The Macmillan Company.

Lose, E., & Lovich, N. P. (Ed.). (2014). *Living on death row.* LFB Scholarly Publishing LLC.

Mannréttindaskrifstofa Íslands Icelandic Human Rights Centre. (n.d.). *The death row phenomenon: Soering v. The United Kingdom.* Mannréttindaskrifstofa Íslands Icelandic Human Rights Centre.

Penal Reform International. (2014, April). *Fighting for client's lives: The impact of the death penalty on defence lawyers.* Penal Reform International.

Sharp, S. F. (2005). *Hidden victims: The effects of the death penalty on families of the accused.* Rutgers University Press.

Snell, T. L. (2021, June). *Capital punishment, 2019 - statistical tables.* U.S. Department of Justice Bureau of Justice Statistics.

Stout, D. G., (1988, February 14). The lawyers of death row. *The New York Times.*

The National Child Traumatic Stress Network. (2021) *Children who are impacted by a family member's death sentence of execution: Information for mental health professionals.* The National Child Traumatic Stress Network.

Vollum, S. (2008). *Last words and the death penalty: Voices of the condemned and their co-victims.* LFB Scholarly Publishing LLC.

Yanofski, J. (2011, Feb). Setting up a death row psychiatry program. *Innovations in Clinical Neuroscience. 8*(2), 19-22.

7
Ethical Implications

by Aleefa Devji

❖

The death penalty has been used as a form of punishment for crimes throughout history. Although the offences punishable by death have varied over the centuries and the severity of torture associated with the act have become more humane, the death penalty is still debated. The long-standing argument of whether the death penalty is in fact immoral is often the focal point of these debates today. This may beg the question, is the death penalty ethically unjust? And what are the arguments for and against the continued use of the death penalty.

Some states and individuals believe that the death penalty is a form of retribution, or a way for closure for the families of victims. On the other hand, others argue that human life itself is valuable and even the most serious crimes should not warrant punishment by taking a life.

Retribution

There are many arguments that support the use of the death penalty. One such argument is that retribution and punishment supports the ideals that all guilty people deserve to be punished and that they should be punished by means proportional to the severity of the crime they committed. The retributive argument also states that in order for justice to be served, people must suffer for their wrongdoing but also in a way that is appropriate and proportional. Thereby, it supports the use of the death penalty for crimes such as murder. An example of state support for the death penalty using the argument for retribution is in the case of Dhananjoy Chatterjee, where the Justices of the Supreme Court of India stated (Chaterjee vs State Of W.B, 1994):

> "The measure of punishment in a given case must depend upon the atrocity of the crime, the conduct of the criminal and the defenseless and unprotected state of the victim. Imposition of appropriate punishment is the manner in which the courts respond to the society's cry for justice against the criminals. Justice demands that the courts should impose punishment befitting the crime so that the courts reflect public abhorrence of the crime."

In simple terms, they are arguing for the punishment for the crime to be dependent on the atrocity of the crime, the nature of the crime, and the ability for the victim to defend or protect themselves. Therefore, support for the use of the death penalty is warranted to reflect the public's despise for the act. Further supporting the retributive rationale behind the death penalty, the argument "an eye for an eye" is often also used (British Broadcasting Corporation [BBC], 2014). Many also argue against retribution as being a morally just argument for the use of the death penalty. The defense against the retributive case is that capital punishment is in fact a form of vengeance rather than retribution as a result of the anticipation of suffering that the criminal will experience. Thereby, it is believed that the years spent on death row awaiting their punishment by death are seen as more severe and inhumane than the actual punishment by death itself.

Deterrence

The idea of deterring others who are inclined to commit heinous crimes with the threat of punishment by death is another argument used to justify the use of the death penalty. Although this argument is seen as valid by some, it is an argument that does not stand up to statistical evidence. Additionally, this argument also fails to take into account the fact that and also does not take into account that some individuals who are subject to capital punishment were not capable of being deterred as a result of mental illness.

The use of the death penalty as a deterrent to further heinous criminality is only effective when the punishment is dealt with soon after the crime is committed. Therefore, the more drawn out the legal process or the time until the punishment is dealt, the less effective the punishment will be as a form of deterrence. This is similar to punishing a child for a consequential action such as touching a hot stove; the immediate pain will teach them not to do it again as the pain is associated with the action. Cardinal Avery Dulles outlines in the religious journal, Catholicism and Capital Punishment (Dulles, 2001):

> Executions, especially where they are painful, humiliating and public, may create a sense of horror that would prevent others from tempting to commit similar crimes… In our day death is usually administered in private by relatively painless means, such as injections of drugs, and to that extent it may be less effective as a deterrent."

Many would argue against the deterrent value of the death penalty, using rationales similar to those of Cardinal Avery Dulles. Historically, the public display of the torture endured by the guilty parties may have provided a deterrent factor but nevertheless there were other ethical issues with the use of this punishment at that time.

Rehabilitation

Another argument used to support the death penalty surrounds the idea of rehabilitation, although not specifically with respect to rehabilitation for return into society. This argument is instead used to support the use of the death penalty as a means for rehabilitation and the express of remorse prior to execution so the individual can escape evil and punishment in the next life.

Prevention of Re-offending

Most individuals would say that prevention of further criminal behaviour by an individual is not a fair or sufficient justification to take a human life, as there are other more ethical means to protect society from re-offenders such as life imprisonment without the possibility of parole. Although, to some who are supportive of the death penalty, life imprisonment alone is not seen as adequate to protect society. In many states the possibility of life imprisonment without the opportunity for parole after 25 years is not seen as ethical or humane in itself (BBC, 2014). For this reason, the death penalty is supported as a means to protect society from criminals because if they are executed they are unable to engage in criminal behaviour again in the future. One may argue that even the protection of society is not enough to say that taking the life of a human is ethically justified.

Arguments Against the Death Penalty and Ethical Concerns

Retribution, deterrence, rehabilitation, and prevention of re-offending are arguments used to support the death penalty, although most if not all of them are met with pushback and concern for the ethical implications associated with the punishment. On the other side of the discussion are the arguments in favor of abolishing the death penalty, or against its reintroduction in States where it has already been abolished. Some of these arguments include the value of a human life, the right to life for every human, the potential execution of the innocent, or arguments against the death penalty with respect to deterrence and retributive justice.

The Value of a Human Life and The Right to Live

A human life is no doubt valuable, and there is support for the belief that even the worst criminals or murderers should not be punished to death because their lives are also of value. This means that even if a person has taken the life of another, the value of their life should not be taken away. From the perspective of religious beliefs and ethical guidelines, there is also an opposition to the death penalty as we as humans are not to play god and therefore do not have the right to take the life of another human.

The value of human life goes hand in hand with human rights, wherein the Charter states that each individual has a right to life. Even the criminally guilty have a right to life, but sentencing them to death violates that fundamental human right. Although some supporters of the death penalty have defended the death penalty against this argument by stating that actions have consequences, and the vile behaviour of a murderer would thereby forfeit their right to life (BBC, 2014). This would be a similar idea to an individual forfeiting their right to live if they attack another individual and the victim kills them in self-defense to save their own life.

Although these two ideals are similar, the latter is in the heat of the moment where no other options are available to the victim, whereas choosing to punish an individual to death after the fact is taking their right to life as opposed to them choosing to forfeit it.

This also brings us back to the ethical implications of the death penalty in terms of timely execution that more often than not does not happen.

Innocent or Guilty

One of the most common and well understood arguments against the death penalty and ethical misconduct is the execution of the innocent. The judicial system is undoubtedly not perfect, and as a result mistakes are often made whether by the system, or bias from the lawyers or jurors. As a result, it is inevitable that innocent people may also be sentenced to death and have their right to life revoked. Despite the support for the death penalty and the belief that taking an individual's life if they have forfeited their right to life is acceptable, in the case of the execution of the innocent, there is no way to repair the wrongdoings of the court system. Therefore, the use of the death penalty poses ethical concerns that go back to the value of a life and that all life should be preserved.

In the United States, there have been many reported incidents of individuals being sentenced to death and later found to be innocent. Specifically, since 1973 there have been 130 people found innocent and released from death row (Amnesty International, 2012). In these cases, the torture and suffering of these individuals cannot be undone but if they were executed before being proved innocent. the 130 lives would have been unfairly and inhumanely revoked.

Issues with the Retributive Defense

As we have learned, retribution is a defense used to support the death penalty as there is a belief that punishment should be proportionate to the severity of the crime. On the opposing side of the debate, there is a belief that retribution is in fact morally and ethically flawed when put in practice. In the US Catholic Conference it was stated that, "we cannot teach that killing is wrong by killing" and this is an earnest statement that points out the flaws in retribution but there are other factors to consider, such as vengeance.

The main argument in the case against the retributive defense is that retribution is a form of vengeance or revenge. Historically, capital punishment has been carried out with the ability for the audience to get their revenge by seeing the criminal tortured, burned, or stoned which garnered some of the support for the death penalty in early times (BBC, 2014). This vindictiveness associated with the retribution is just one reason that retribution is not a strong enough defense against the ethical implications of capital punishment.

Going back to the lives of the innocents who have been sentenced to death, we can understand that the retributive defense would also not hold. As the judicial system can be flawed and mistakes can possibly be made, there is a high chance that innocent individuals can be executed. Although the act would be by mistake, it would still violate one of the main principles of retribution that people should get what they deserve. Ethically, this is concerning because this wrongdoing can not be made right, as innocent life cannot be spared once taken awake by means of execution, and if not yet executed the trauma of death row would be irreversible.

Brutality of the Death Penalty

Another argument supporting the morally flawed use of the death penalty is the brutalization of individuals and society. Statistics actually show that more murders actually take place in states where capital punishment is utilized, compared to states where its use has been abolished. This may be a result of individuals who are angered by the possibility of execution being driven to commit the serious crimes that will be met with capital punishment. Arguments in support of the death penalty may utilize deterrence to support their position, but this statistical evidence based on data from the Federal Bureau of Investigations reportings, the death penalty fails to deter serious and violent crimes. More often than not it is the chance or likelihood of being caught and punished for the crime that is the deterring factor (BBC, 2014). The brutalization associated with the death penalty also affects society and the state's relationship with it's citizens. The ability for a state to have the power to execute an individual for their behaviour creates conflict, as it is a display of the state having the power and free will to do anything that it pleases. The power that the state has to take the lives of individuals, despite their criminal acts, is demoralizing and can lead to a state being seen as uncivilized. For example, civilized societies should not tolerate torture, even if there is deterrent value in the torturous act or if the act is seen as an eye for an eye. As Cesare Becarria stated in 1764, "murder that is depicted as a horrible crime is repeated in cold blood, remorsely (Beccaria, 1794)." Beccaria is right, because in a civilized society there should be no good reason to allow torture of an individual, even if they are responsible for a heinous crime. Repeating the act in cold blood makes the state no better than the individual, as they are using their power to punish and play god by choosing who should live and who can be put to death.

Unfair Application of Capital Punishment

In some states that utilize the death penalty, there is concern that flaws within the judicial system will make the application of the death penalty unfair. For example one Supreme Court Justice who was originally in favour of the death penalty eventually changed their stance and came to the conclusion that, "the death penalty remains fraught with arbitrariness, discrimination, caprice, and mistake... Experience has taught up that the constitutional goal of eliminating arbitrariness and discrimination from the administration of death... can never be achieved without compromising an equally essential component of fundamental fairness - individualized sentencing (Hood & Hoyle, 2015)." From this statement made by Justice Harry Blackmun, an important and key idea is brought up about individualized sentencing, as no two crimes are the same and the circumstances upon which they were committed may not be the same. Therefore, how and why is it fair for the state to use capital punishment for all crimes that seemingly meet the criteria for execution.

In other aspects of the criminal justice system, such as with jurors and lawyers, there may also be flaws that lead to unfair use of capital punishment. For example, jurors in many of the US death penalty cases must be "death eligible" which means that the juror must be willing to convict the individual on trial knowing that there is a possibility the accused will be sentenced to death. By requiring that prospective jury members are "death eligible" the US court system is thereby creating a jury biased in favour of the death penalty. Another major flaw in the justice system is concerning lawyers or legal aid provided to individuals who are unable to afford a lawyer of their own. In 66% of cases where offenders are provided with legal aid lawyers, there can be an expectation that they will be sentenced to death, but this percentage can drop to as low as 25% if the defendant is able to afford a lawyer of their own choosing (BBC, 2014).

Capital Punishment is Inhumane, Degrading and Unnecessary

The arguments against the death penalty and the suffering and torture that accused individuals encounter both on death row and through the means of execution are seen as inhumane. Many of the methods used for execution cause enormous amounts of pain and suffering, such as the use of lethal gas, electrocution, or even strangulation. Throughout history other methods of execution were also used but have been abandoned because they were seen as too barbaric or required too much "hands-on" force by the executioner. Some such methods included the use of firing squads or even the beheading of the accused (BBC, 2014).

In many countries where capital punishment is still used, the method of lethal injections has now been adopted because it is seen as less cruel or torturous for the offender, and reduces the brutalizing nature for the executioner (BBC, 2014). In opposition to this method, those who are against the use of capital punishment would argue that lethal injection is also a method that should be abandoned because it is also morally flawed. The moral implications associated with the use of lethal injection stem from the fact that medical personnel are required to be directly involved in the execution of the individual rather than just being the one to pronounce them dead. Therefore, this is fundamentally and medically unethical as medical professionals take an oath to do no harm, and to not play a god by partaking in acts that would take the life of a human. Secondly, the use of lethal injection is morally flawed and inhumane as post-mortem findings have indicated that the levels of anesthetic agents found in the offenders were consistent with awakening during the procedure and the ability to experience pain.

Another argument against the death penalty and the ethical implications associated with capital punishment is once which is more politically driven and stems from the political principle that the state should fulfill its obligations by the least invasive, harmful and restrictive means possible (BBC, 2014). The state is obligated to punish individuals for the crimes they have committed in order to preserve societal conduct and safety for its citizens, but in doing so, the political principle would argue for the least harmful means to be used. From this political stance, capital punishment does not fulfill this principle but instead it is seen as the most harmful punishment that is readily available, so it should only be used in cases where no punishment that is less harmful is appropriate or available. It can be argued that in all cases of punishment for heinous crimes there will always be an alternative method for the state to fulfill its objective while abiding by the principle of using the least invasive and harmful means. Therefore, it can be argued even on a political front that the use of capital punishment is unethical and even for the most serious crimes the use of execution poses ethical implications for society.

Conclusion

To conclude this discussion on the ethical implications of the death penalty and execution of the criminally guilty, it is imperative that there is an understanding for both sides of the argument. As the death penalty has not been fully abolished throughout the world, it is still in use in many states and countries which all utilize different means for execution. The continued use of capital punishment creates a platform for debate surrounding the death penalty and the ethical implications of its use. Although many may find that there are arguments for the use of the death penalty, such as its retributive value and the possibility for deterrence, there are also many arguments against the death penalty and the ethical implications that are posed to society and individuals even if there is value in its use. Similarly, there are many arguments that support the abolition of the death penalty based on the ethical and immoral implications that are posed but these are oftentimes not seen as universal arguments, and may not hold up against the views of all states and countries around the world. Therefore, the death penalty is a topic that has been debated throughout history and will hopefully continue to be debated until its use is entirely abolished.

References

Amnesty International. (2012, May). Death Penalty Facts.

BBC. (2014). *Ethics - capital punishment: Arguments in favour of capital punishment.* Ethics Guide.

BBC. (2014). *Ethics - capital punishment: Arguments against capital punishment.* Ethics Guide.

Beccaria, C. (1794). *An essay on crimes and punishments* (No. 47183). Philip H. Nicklin.

Dhananjoy Chaterjee vs State Of W.B

Dulles, A. C. (2001). Catholicism & Capital Punishment. First Things, 30-35.

Hood, R., & Hoyle, C. (2015). The death penalty: A worldwide perspective. OUP Oxford.

Walter, L. (2019, January 10). *The death penalty: Going beyond moral arguments.* The Death Penalty: Going Beyond Moral Arguments.

8

Stay of Execution

By Alexa Gee

This chapter will discuss what a stay of execution is in the context of the death penalty. Information will focus on how a stay of execution applies to the American justice system since Canada and many other countries have abolished the death penalty. First, a stay of execution will be defined. Then, reasons for a stay of execution will be established. Finally, this chapter will highlight stays of executions in countries outside the United States.

What is a Stay of Execution?

A stay of execution is an order commanding that the execution be stopped until further proceedings (Gressman, 1986). Granting an appeal is subject to judicial discretion. In the Supreme Court, a single justice can decide, although an appellant can apply for the entire Court to consider the stay of execution. Before asking for a stay of execution from a higher court, a litigator must exhaust all other possibilities in the lower court.

A stay of execution does not just apply to the death penalty (Cornell Law School, n.d.). It can also mean stopping the sale of a property, but this chapter will focus on how it applies solely to the death penalty.

Once granted, the stay of execution has a specific time window (Shergroup, n.d.). It must be accompanied by an immediate order to stop the enforcement, typically for 24-48 hours. This allows for more time for a more in-depth review of the sentence, as the court may take days to weeks to decide how to proceed. A stay of execution can last for 30 days. Since 1976, 294 people in the United States have been granted clemency (CNN, n.d.).

Stay of executions are closely tied with applying for appeals and calls for a new trial (Cornell Law School, n.d.). The appellant must demonstrate that the appeal is not frivolous and is a genuine issue that is arguable in court (Kimani et al., 2021). Applying for an appeal or being granted an appeal does not automatically create a stay of execution (Gexall, 2014). A stay of execution must be applied for, which the court will only grant if there is a compelling reason to do so. There are certain conditions that must be followed, such as a payment of a predetermined sum.

In the past five years, out of 80 execution dates, 32 were stayed by federal courts (Tcadp.org, n.d.). Granting a stay of execution is not rare, but in many of these cases, the execution is simply rescheduled for a later date (Death Penalty Information Centre, n.d.). A stay of execution can be granted at the last minute, like in Melissa Lucio's case discussed later in this chapter, which happened within 48 hours (Sklar, 2012).

The United States currently has executions for federal inmates paused under the Biden administration (The Associated Press, 2022; Walsh, 2021). Previously, the Trump administration had resumed these executions, which had been paused prior to his presidency for 17 years (The Associated Press, 2022). Merrick Garland ordered the federal government to hold off on all executions in 2021 (Walsh, 2021). For federal death row inmates, the president is the only one who has the power to grant a pardon.

Reasons for a Stay of Execution

Courts have broad discretion when issuing a stay of execution (Sklar, 2012). However, capital punishment sentencing is held to a higher safeguard than other sentences to try to minimize the arbitration of the death penalty. A stay of execution can be granted on the grounds that there was a denial of a constitutional right, legal acts coming into conflict, if more time is needed to analyze the merits of the appeal, *habeas corpus*, a significant chance that the court will reverse their original decision, or if the method of execution could cause "severe pain." There are several other reasons that have popped up throughout history; sometimes no explanation is disclosed as to why the stay of execution was granted. There are no formal rules that the court has to follow when granting a stay of execution, though there are guidelines in some cases.

Denial of a Constitutional Right

If a person's constitutional rights are denied during prison or the justice process, this can be grounds for a stay of execution (Sklar, 2012). Many foreign nationals have been sentenced to death in the United States without legal resources from national consulates when arrested (Sklar, 2012). In many legal circles, this could be considered a violation of the Vienna Convention on Consular Relations, but the Supreme Court has said that failure to meet these rights is not enough grounds to grant a stay of execution. In Medellin v. Texas, a Mexican national was not informed of his right to communicate with the Mexican consulate. It is not uncommon for this to happen, as pointed out that at least 51 other Mexican nationals have been denied these rights around the same time as Medellin v. Texas. A stay of execution was granted to a prisoner on death row after several inmates sought damages over the disclosure of private letters citing a breach of confidence and nominal damages for copyright infringement (Lum, 2022).

Stanely Faulder, a Canadian native of Jasper, Alberta was awarded a stay of execution in Texas after being convicted of the robbery and murder of an elderly Texan woman (O'Hara, 2018). He had been awarded a stay of execution nine times in total, granted on the grounds that his right to contact Canadian diplomats was violated when he was arrested. This was said to be a violation of the Vienna Convention on Consular Relations, like in Medellin v. Texas. Like this previous case, Faulder was eventually executed after a 24-year battle to overturn his sentence (CBC News, 2000). He was the first Canadian to be executed in the United States since 1952.

Legal Acts

Certain legal acts that come into conflict may be cause for a stay of execution (Sklar, 2012). In Rosenberg v. the United States, for example, two defendants alleged that the Atomic Energy Act of 1946 superseded the Espionage Act. Ultimately, this meant that the District Court did not have the jurisdiction to impose a death sentence. In Gardner v. Florida, a stay of execution was granted due to the pending decision of the Supreme Court as to whether Florida's capital sentencing procedure was constitutional. It is important for the justice system to recognize and apply, retroactively, new rules regarding criminal procedures (Sharp, 2022).

James David Autry, who was strapped to the execution table, was granted a stay of execution based on whether his sentence was proportional to other similar crimes (Taylor, 1984). Autry had murdered a convenience store owner during a robbery. His execution was rescheduled, but it was decided that this argument was not enough grounds for appeal and he was put to death.

More Time Needed

When there is new evidence to consider, more time may be needed to determine how this influences the court's decision. Several high-profile cases have caught the attention of international news (The Associated Press, 2022). For example, in Texas, Melissa Lucio was found guilty of beating her two-year-old daughter to death. Her case attracted the attention of many celebrities, more than half the members of the Texas legislature, and jurors of the original trial who called for a stay of execution. New evidence was revealed that looked at the nature of her daughter's injuries; bruising was consistent with falling down the stairs rather than beating. The Texas Board of Pardons and Paroles are the ones who hear a request to commute the death sentence and can change it to life in prison. They are also able to give a 120-day execution reprieve. As of 2022, Melissa Lucia has won a stay of execution and her death sentence has not been carried out.

Habeas Corpus

A petition invoking Habeas Corpus as the reason to grant a stay of execution is when there is unlawful detention and imprisonment (Sklar, 2012). To invoke habeaus corpus, the appellant must demonstrate substantial grounds for this claim.

Ed Johnson was the first African American granted a stay of execution by the United States Supreme Court (The Ed Johnson Project, n.d.). Ed Johnson was convicted of rape in 1906 in Chatanooga, Tennessee, although his innocence is debated (Linder, n.d.). Johnson made a petition for a "writ of habeas corpus" because his trial lacked a fair and impartial jury. He was arrested based on the accusation of a white man, who collected a monetary reward for capturing the perpetrator. He was also said to have been denied several constitutional rights. His petition was denied by the state of Tennessee. This was the first time that the US Supreme Court became involved in a state case, after the local city of Chattanooga,

Tennessee ignored the stay of execution (The Ed Johnson Project, n.d.). Unfortunately, ire from white southerners who opposed the Supreme Court's decision sparked a mob that stormed the jail Johnson was held in, wrestling in Johnson being lynched to death. Following Johnson's death, 2 men were tried for contempt of court for ignoring the stay of execution establishing the seriousness of following this order in the United States (Linder, n.d.).

Reversal of Decision

The strength of a person's claim is a good way to predict if a decision is likely to be reversed (Di Francesco, 2021). If it is believed that the death penalty was likely to be reversed in the subsequent proceedings following a stay of execution, they were more likely to issue a stay of execution. Also, it is based on the probability that the claimant can pay the required sum associated with the new trial.

The Execution Method

In South Carolina, an execution that was to be carried out by the firing squad was halted (Allen, 2022). Richard Moore, convicted of murdering a store clerk, was given the death penalty. However, South Carolina struggled to obtain lethal injection drugs, since pharmaceutical companies are reluctant to sell medication for execution. The rules allow for the use of the gas chamber or electric chair in the event medication cannot be acquired. The South Carolina Department of Correction was sued due to the fact that these latter methods violate South Carolina's constitution, which explicitly bars cruel or unusual punishments.

In a bold case, it was argued that the stay of execution itself is a cruel and unusual punishment (McCleand, 2015). Richard Glossip has been on death row for the last 25 years in Oklahoma, having his execution date moved three times (Ehrlich, 2021). 35 days before their execution, the prisoner is transferred to a new cell, called

Death Watch, where they stay for one week. Prisoners are then transferred to a cell closer to the execution chamber, where they can sometimes observe inmates walking to their death past the cell. Glossip has stated that he could hear inmates being put to death, where complications with lethal injections draw out the process. Having to repeat this process three times, where the stay of execution arrived near moments before it was scheduled to happen, could be classified as torture (McCleand, 2015). The most recent stay of execution was because they used the wrong chemicals, potassium acetate, instead of potassium chloride (Ehrlich, 2021). This process certainly takes a toll on mental health when one has to mentally prepare for their death again and again, uncertain if it will be the last time (McCleand, 2015). Currently, Glossip is still awaiting an execution; in the meantime, he is fighting to end this process.

Other Unique Cases

In the case of a temporary halting of the execution of Alabama man Willie Smith, the Supreme Court ruled that if a priest/chaplain was in the room, the execution could not take place (France 24, 2021). This was on the grounds that they could not interfere with the practice of religious faith.

Veron Madison received a stay of execution in the state of Alabama after it was determined he was mentally incompetent and had no memory of the offence (Death Penalty Information Center, n.d.). The 67-year-old had suffered several strokes that left him with brain damage, an inability to walk, and dementia.

Several stays of execution have been granted because of COVID-19 in 2020, either because the inmate scheduled to be executed contracted COVID-19 or because of the widespread conditions of the virus sweeping through the prison (Death Penalty Information Center, n.d.).

International Cases

Singapore

Sometimes multiple governments and countries will get involved in requesting a stay of execution (United Nations, 2022). As seen in the cases above for the Denial of Constitutional Rights section. Outside the United States, countries that still have the death penalty may have to face the governments of others. For example, the Malaysian government requested Singapore to halt the execution of a Malaysian national, Nagaenthran Dharmalingam, who was found guilty of drug trafficking, with the United Nations echoing the sentiments of the Malaysian government. Dharmalingam was granted a stay of execution in Singapore because he had tested positive for Covid 19 (Lin, 2021). Ultimately, Singapore still went ahead with the execution. Two days after Dharmalingam was hanged, another Malaysian national charged with a drug offence, Datchinamurthy Kataiah, was granted a stay of execution (Bernama, 2022). As of May 2022, his sentence has not been carried out.

Iran

A high-profile case was the trial and execution of Makwan Mouloudzadeh, who was convicted of rape in 2000 in Iran (Talt, 2007). A judiciary chief had requested a stay of execution on the grounds that the sentence did not conform to Sharia law. Mouloudzadeh was a minor at the time of the crime and during the trial, the accusers withdrew their allegations; Mouloudzadeh also retracted his confession. There was a lack of evidence as well, but Mouloudzadeh was still found guilty. Mouloudzadeh was executed in 2007. Human Rights Watch condemned Iran for ignoring the stay of execution order and for its treatment of juvenile offenders.

In a similar case that caught the attention of the United Nations, Hossein Shahbazi was found guilty of the murder of a classmate during a fight when he was 17 (United Nations, 2022). Shabazi was denied a lawyer after his arrest and there were reports that his confession was obtained under torture. A stay of execution was granted with international law cited, which forbids the death penalty on those under 18 being brought up. As of May 2022, he has not been executed.

In a case citing a unique law, an Iranian woman was granted a stay of execution (Amnesty International, 2009). Akram Mahdavi murdered her abusive husband in 2003. She was scheduled to be executed in 2008 but under Article 264 of the Iranian Penal code, a blood relative of the murder victim can pardon the guilty in exchange for compensation. Mahdavi's execution was postponed so her family could collect diyeh, blood money, as compensation.

Pakistan

Shafqat Hussain was charged with involuntary manslaughter when he was 14 years old, and was given a stay of execution after human rights groups pointed out the various injustices of his trial (BBC News, 2015). He was tried by Pakistan's anti-terrorism courts, even though his charge was not related to terrorism. There were also reports of Hussain confessing under duress.

Pakistan has also stayed the execution of a man diagnosed with schizophrenia, although Pakistan's Supreme Court had initially rejected the petition (NDTV, 2016). After being visited by a psychiatrist, it was determined he could not be treated for paranoid schizophrenia.

In a dispute with India, the United Nations court ordered Pakistan to stay the execution of Kulbhushan Jadhav (AlJazeera, 2017). A Pakistani military court sentenced him to death in 2017, charging him with espionage and sabotage. Jadhav was denied access to the Indian consulate, which is a right according to the Vienna Convention on Consular Relations, on the grounds that this was a case of national security. India has denied that Jadhav is a spy and turned to the United Nations International Court of Justice for help in releasing him. The International Court of Justice's rules are final and binding, but they cannot enforce their rules. As of May 2022, he has not been executed.

Australia

In 1962, it was found that the trial judge was obligated to issue a stay of execution when a person was found insane at the time of execution (Feltham, 1964). However, prior to this, a prima facie case of insanity must be established first. This was the case for Robert Peters Tait who appealed to the Victorian Court of Criminal Appeal; later, when that appeal was dismissed he applied to the High Court of Australia (Feltham, 1964; Richards, 2012). When that too did not stop his execution, an application was made to the High Court. The Mental Health Act 1959, scheduled to start applying on the day Tait was to be hanged, helped define the concept of "mentally ill or intellectually defective." This law saved Tait from execution after a last minute stay of execution ordered by the chief justice (Richards, 2012).

Conclusion

This chapter discussed what a stay of execution is, in the context of the death penalty. Unique cases within the American justice system that led to a stay of execution were highlighted to explain the parameters and guidelines surrounding this order. Aside from the United States, examples of other areas where a stay of execution has been issued, including Singapore, Iran, Pakistan, and Australia, were explored. This is not an exhaustive list of where a stay of execution happens, there are many countries that still have the death penalty that grant a stay of execution.

References

Al Jazeera. (2017, May 18). *ICJ orders Pakistan to stay execution of Indian 'spy'.* News | Al Jazeera.

BBC News. (2015, January 5). *Pakistan grants Shafqat Hussain stay of execution.* BBC News.

CBC news. (2000, November 11). *Faulder executed in Texas | CBC news.*

Chambers, H. D. F. B. at K., & Francesco, H. D. (2021, July 21). *Stays of execution in adjudication enforcement: When are the merits of the underlying claim relevant?* Construction Blog.

Death Penalty Information Center. (2021). *Chattanooga dedicates memorial to Ed Johnson, an innocent man sentenced to death on false rape charges and lynched after U.S. Supreme Court stayed his execution.* Death Penalty Information Center.

Ehrlich, B. (2021, September 7). *Richard Glossip v. the death machine.* Rolling Stone.

Feltham, J. F. (1964). *the common law and the execution of insane criminals.*

Linder, D. O. (n.d.). *The Supreme Court intervenes in the ed johnson case.* Famous Trials.

NDTV. (2016, October 31). *Pakistan Supreme Court stays execution of schizophrenic death row convict.* NDTV.com.

O'Hara, J. (2018). *Faulder gets stay of execution.* The Canadian Encyclopedia.

Richards, M. (2012, December 11). *Tait, Robert Peters (1924–1985).* Biography - Robert Peters Tait.

Sklar, R. (2012). Executing equity: The broad judicial discretion to stay the execution ... *Hofstra Law Review, 40*(3), 770–809.

Tait, R. (2007, December 7). *Stay of execution fails to save Iranian man.* The Guardian.

United Nations. (2022). *Experts urge Iran to halt imminent execution of juvenile offender | | UN news.* United Nations.

9

Public Support for the Death Penalty

by Irene Falade

✣

Why do people support the death penalty?

The subject of the death penalty is a very controversial one all around the world. Many people have opinions on it, most of it differing strongly from another; hence why there is no general consensus on whether or not the death penalty is a good or bad policy. This chapter will be discussing the support for the death penalty, the good some people see in it, the necessity the believe it has to society, and so on.

Supporters of the death penalty believe that according to social equilibrium, punishment restores the scales of justice that have been violated by someone breaking the laws of society (Pojman & Reiman, 1997, p.10-11). What this means is that there is a social equilibrium of burdens and benefits that delivers justice to society by taking from the criminal what they unfairly got and now owe; so it is that they are demanding their debt. (Pojman & Reiman, 1997,

127

p.10-11). According to Pojman & Reiman (1997), this is known as the Morris unfair advantage or fair play argument for supporters of the death penalty (p.11). And what they are essentially arguing for is that society has the duty to punish offenders of the law because it also has the duty of resolving unfair advantages within society if possible (Pojman & Reiman, 1997, p.10-11). This argument puts the burden on society as a whole to determine a fitting punishment for individuals who are stepping out of line and basically cheating on the system that everyone else abides by in order to maintain the status quo. In addition to the fair play argument held by death penalty endorsers, there are many other positions they take when defending their support for the use of the death penalty, such as the retributivist position, deterrence argument, and moral justification.

With the retributivist position, Pojman & Reiman (1997) explain it as any criminal that commits murder must die, because there is no other suitable punishment that can fully deliver justice for such a crime when death and living the most miserable life cannot be compared (p.29). Meaning that there has to be equality between the crime and justice served, and by not putting said criminal death as punishment under the law, that means there is a lack of equality occurring (Pojman & Reiman, 1997, p.29). And by committing a murder, taking away the life of another person, the murderer themselves have forfeited their right to live under the state's law because Pojman (1997) states that the right to life is not an absolute right the state is in violation of by seeking justice (p.30). In addition to that, Pojman (1997), argues that if a human's right to life was truly absolute, then individuals could not kill their aggressors under the act of self-defence (p.30). And more so, the right to life is a conditional one that can and should be overridden when it comes to the subject matter of a bigger or more important moral reasoning (Pojman & Reiman, 1997, p.30). As Pojman (1997) claims, "Every person's right to life, liberty and property is connected to our duty to respect that of others in society and when we violate those rights of others we also forfeit our own rights", which can be broken down to a simple understanding of violating one's right to life means the perpetrator in kind forfeits their own right to life (p.30). Furthermore, this retributivist position argues for the principle of 'just desserts', which is meant to emphasize that not only does a criminal that has committed murder revoked their right to live but they also deserve the capital punishment of death similar to the moral justification position also used by death penalty supporter but will be further discussed later (Pojman & Reiman, 1997, p.30). As Pojman (1997) puts it, "committing a capital offence means deserving a capital crime" (p.30).

Followed by the retributivist position, is the fabled deterrence argument of death penalty supporters. The mindset behind the deterrence argument is that the existence of the death penalty protects innocent lives by preventing convicted or probable murderers from killing (Bedau & Cassell, 2004, p.187). Supporters of the death penalty believe that first degree murders, the only type eligible for capital punishment, can be deterred by having the death penalty in place (Pojman & Reiman, 1997). Deterrence falls into two categories according to Bedau & Cassell (2004), general deterrence and specific deterrence (p.189). General deterrence is a case where the death penalty's restraining effect affects the larger population that includes potential murderers by dissuading them from committing the crime (Bedau & Cassell, 2004, p.189). While specific deterrence is where the incapacitative benefits of the death penalty prevents already convicted and apprehended murderers from killing once again (Bedau & Cassell, 2004, p.189).

Bedau and Cassell (2004), give examples for both, first with specific deterrence the case of Kenneth Allen McDuff, who killed and raped a woman after escaping execution and being released from prison in 1989 (183-185). McDuff is the perfect example of specific deterrence because If the abolitionists had failed to obtain a temporary moratorium on death penalties from 1972 to 1976, he would have been executed, and Colleen Reed and many other young women would've been alive today (Bedau & Cassell, 2004, p.187-188). For general deterrence, there is evidence from criminals who have committed an offence punishable by life imprisonment held back from killing when at risk of capture, even though by killing, they might have been able to get away (Pojman & Reiman, 1997, p.48). And according to Pojman & Reiman (1997) the reason given by criminals when asked why they refrained from the homicide, is that they would rather serve the life sentence than risk getting a death penalty (p.48). More evidence of the death penalty deterrence benefits is explained, "...by the fact that out of roughly 52,000 state prison inmates serving time for murder, an estimated 810 had previously been convicted of murder and had killed 821 persons following those convictions. Executing each of these inmates after the first murder conviction would have saved the lives of more than 800 persons. "(Bedau & Cassell, 2004, p.188). These serve to strongly support the death penalty deterrence argument as a number of innocent lives could have been spared if the death penalty was still in place or had the executions been followed through.

However, the death penalty does not serve as deterrence for all murders, according to Bedau & Cassell (2004), it only applies to certain types of murders which have to meet the criteria of requiring reflection and forethought by persons of reasonable intelligence and unimpaired mental faculties (p.189). These type of murders as determined by the supreme court, are deemed first degree murders and premeditated with malice meaning it was planned and thought out beforehand rather than being spur of the moment or self-defense (Bedau & Cassell, 2004, p.190). So supporters for this argument and the death penalty emphasize that deterrence isn't about dissuading every possible murder deter but only some within their power (Bedau & Cassell, 2004, p.190). To wrap up the deterrence position, here is a statement made by Professor James Q. Wilson to explain why the death penalty does have a deterrence factor,

People are governed in their daily lives by rewards and penalties of every sort. We shop for bargain prices, praise our children for good behaviour and scold them for bad, expect lower interest rates to stimulate home building and fear that higher ones will depress it, and conduct ourselves in public in ways that lead our friends and neighbours to form good opinions of us. To assert that 'deterrence doesn't work' is tantamount to either denying the plainest facts of everyday life or claiming that would-be criminals are utterly different from the rest of us (Bedau & Cassell. 2004, p.189).

The third and final position held by supporters of the death penalty is known as the moral justification argument. According to Pew Research Center (2021), people's support for the death penalty is strongly tied to the belief that when someone commits murder, the death penalty is a morally justified punishment. This is similar to the retributivist position mentioned earlier, where the principle of 'just desert' states that committing a capital crime means deserving a capital punishment (Pojman & Reiman, 1997, p.30). This position is strongly supported among the general public, with 64% of people agreeing that the death penalty is morally justified in cases of murder (Pew Research Center, 2021). While among death penalty supporters there is a whooping 90% of them that believe the death penalty is justified under those circumstances (Pew Research Center, 2021). The Pew Research Center (2021) also found that, "Republicans are 29 percentage points more likely than Democrats to say the death penalty is morally justified, 28 points more likely to say it deters serious crimes, and 19 points more likely to say that adequate safeguards exist to make sure innocents will not be put to death under the penalty". These statistics represent the support held by the public when it comes to morally justifying the death penalty. Along with the other arguments made by supporters of the death penalty that have been discussed, it can be seen that these individuals truly believe in the necessity of continuing to use the death penalty in today's justice system.

A Study: Who supports the death penalty?

When it comes to the discussion of who supports the death penalty, there is an overwhelming focus on the White American population that tends to be on the frontlines of this side of the debate. This section will be looking at a study run by Joe Soss, Laura Langbein, and Alan R. Metelko in 2003 to get a better understanding of why white Americans seem to support the death penalty more than any other race, nationality, or ethnic group. In the U.S. support for the death penalty from the public has varied over time; however, at the time of the study, most people, at least 68%, were in favour of the death penalty (Soss et al., 2003). It is observed that white people have remained the most copious, politically powerful racial group in America even with remarkable shifts in the demographic and political landscape (Soss et al., 2003). They even make up the central support for capital punishment in the U.S., way more than racial minorities (Soss et al., 2003). According to Soss et al. (2003), many observers have claimed that the support white Americans have for executions is driven by distinctive forces that get obscured in analyses that just show average effects across social groups. Soss and colleagues (2003), are specifically interested in how or if racial attitudes might be stoking the white desire for capital punishment in the justice system. Their analysis looks at the white American death penalty support as the product of four factors, which are racial attitudes, social group differences, core values and political attitudes, and features of social context (Soss et al., 2003). The factor of racial attitudes is an especially important one because in the U.S., crime has become an increasingly racialized problem (Soss et al., 2003). Soss et al. (2003), explain that the symbolic link between race and crime in America is not only a reflection of the high violence rates in poor black neighbourhoods, but also of the race-coded rhetoric public officials constantly wield when talking about crime and media coverage to exaggerate black violence. Stories seen in American media regularly convey threatening images of black crime suspects and disproportionately show black prisoners as "irrational, incorrigible, predatory, and dangerous" (Soss et al., 2003). It is because of this that Soss et al. (2003), believe that white Americans tend to associate crime or being a criminal with people of color/racial minorities especially black people. In addition to this, it is also thought that white Americans tend to frame the issues of crime and punishment in racial terms, which has led reporters to argue that the preferences white Americans have for harsh sentencing should be seen as their response to racially colored perceptions of threat (Soss et al., 2003). Soss et al. (2003), consider that harsh punishments might be providing white Americans with a way to control or suppress black people or otherwise grant them a means to vent their anti-black resentments. Soss et al. (2003), provide evidence from previous research that supports this position; from Gilliam and Iyengar in 2000 and Hurwitz and Peffley in 1997, white people that had anti-black stereotypes when shown images of black perpetrators, were more likely to believe they were guilty, more likely to expect recidivism, and more likely to favour harsh criminal punishments. Furthermore, found in mock jury studies were evidence that white jurors were far more likely to inflict the death penalty on black defendants than white ones, and their reasoning for these decisions were ridden with stereotype-consistent justifications (Soss et al., 2003).

To continue on with the study from Soss and colleagues (2003), they used a prejudice scale designed to capture both the cognitive and affective components of anti-black racial attitudes to measure anti-black sentiments in the white American participants. Soss et al. (2003) had the scale made up of three measures of group stereotyping and one measure of group-based antipathy, their stereotype items were used to indicate differences between white respondents' ratings of white and black people on traits of intelligence, laziness, and propensity toward violence and their affective measure was a standard feeling thermometer score indicating how "warm" or "cool" white respondents felt toward black people. Soss and colleagues (2003) explained their hypothesis, "We expect white support for the death penalty to vary across social groups defined by gender, formal education, family income, and religion". The study focused on many factors to be tested, however one factor that stood out was that of death penalty as a matter of trust, which Soss et al. (2003) claimed no previous survey research has analyzed before. Death penalty as a matter of trust was that, there was an emphasis on the difference between trust in people versus trust in the government (Soss et al., 2003). The researchers believed that people with higher level of interpersonal trust tended to have higher level of civic engagement in a variety of domains and they also tended to have stronger commitments to the rights of others, meaning that they were more likely to support the death penalty than other white Americans (Soss et al., 2003). Soss and colleagues (2003) tested their hypothesis with survey data from the 1992 ANES and contextual data from the 1990 U.S. Census. The summary of this study's findings was that among white Americans, racial prejudice ranked the highest in influence on death penalty than any of the other factors (Soss et al., 2003). Soss et al. (2003) state, "white people who express the highest levels of anti-black prejudice are very likely to show strong support for the death penalty under any racial context (.86 in an all-white county); there is little room for escalation". These results validate their hypothesis on white Americans reasoning behind supporting the death penalty more than any other racial group in the country.

Countries in Support of Death Penalty

Crime Rates
This section will be switching the focus from individuals and the general public's support for the death penalty to the countries still in support of the capital punishment. While a lot of countries in the recent era have abandoned the use of the death penalty, there are still many others that still have it as a part of their justice system. According to the Death Penalty Info center, capital punishment as a law and/or practice has been abolished in around 70% of

countries in the world (World Population Review, 2022). Similar data reported by Amnesty International states that at the end of 2020, 108 countries had abolished the death penalty in law for all crimes, 144 countries had abolished the death penalty in law or practice, 28 countries had effectively abolished the death penalty by not executing anyone in the past 10 years, and 55 countries still retained the death penalty for ordinary crimes (World Population Review, 2022). While it appears the death penalty has fallen out of favor among most countries, there are still some that believe in its necessity. A chart below shows the names of these countries and the status of the death penalty there as of 2022 according to World Population Review (2022).

Countries in Support of the Death Penalty

Legal — legal, in use
Rare — legal, no executions in 10+ years
Serious — legal, only used in extreme cases

Legal	Rare	Serious
Afghanistan	Algeria	Brazil
Antigua and Barbuda	Brunei	Burkina Faso
Bahamas	Cameroon	Chile
Bahrain	Central Africa Republic	El Salvador
Bangladesh	Eritrea	Guatemala
Barbados	Eswatini	Israel

Legal	Rare	Serious
Belarus	Ghana	Kazakhstan
Belize	Grenada	Peru
Botswana	Kenya	
China	Laos	
Comoros	Liberia	
Cuba	Malawi	
Dominica	Maldives	
DR Congo	Mali	
Egypt	Mauritania	
Equatorial Guinea	Morocco	
Ethiopia	Myanmar	
Gambia	Niger	
Guyana	Papua New Guinea	
India	Russia	
Indonesia	Sierra Leone	
Iran	South Korea	
Iraq	Sri Lanka	

Legal	Rare	
Jamaica	Tajikistan	
Japan	Tanzania	
Jordan	Tonga	
Kuwait	Tunisia	
Lebanon	Western Sahara	
Lesotho	Zambia	
Libya		
Malaysia		
Nigeria		
North Korea		
+23 more...		

According to the chart, a lot of countries that still support the death penalty make frequent use of it to serve justice to select criminals. It raises the question of whether their reason behind it is due to possibly high crime rates and by making use of the death penalty so often they are attempting to deter others from committing severe crimes. Another chart will be shown below listing the crime index of some of countries that still retain their death penalty, the information gotten from Numbeo's 2022 update.

Crime Index of Death Penalty Countries

Range: -20 being lowest, 80+ being highest

Countries	Crime Index
Brazil	67.01
China	29.39
Chile	53.98
Egypt	46.57
Iraq	46.95
Israel	32.12
Jamaica	67.84
Nigeria	63.84
North Korea	60.28
Singapore	27.64
South Korea	26.49
Puerto Rico	62.20
Russia	39.62
USA	48.16

Unfortunately, a clear conclusion cannot be drawn from the crime index represented and the possible impact death penalty might have on it as many other factors in those countries could play a role.

Canada Support for Death Penalty

Canada is among one of the many countries that have abolished the death penalty; however, this does not mean everybody in the nation agrees with that decision. There are many people who believe in the use of the death penalty and support it, one of the most notable figures being former Prime Minister Stephen Harper who has openly shown support for the death penalty (Amnesty International, n.d.). Former Prime Minister Harper is not alone in the sentiment of wanting Canada to bring back the death penalty, a recent survey by Research co. (2022) shows. An online survey of a representative national sample was taken and 51% of Canadians are in full support of the death penalty reinstatement (Research co., 2022). Research co.'s (2022), broke down the results with these statistics showing that support for capital punishment is highest among Canadians aged 55 and over (55%) followed closely by those aged 35-to-54 (51%). It was also found that, "more than three-in-five Canadians who voted for the Conservative Party in last year's federal election (63%) are in favour of reinstating the death penalty for murder in Canada, along with 52% of those who supported the New Democratic Party (NDP) and 49% of those who cast ballots for Liberal Party candidates" (Research co., 2022). These survey results show a rising support for the death penalty in Canada among the general population.

According to Mario Canseco, the president of Research Co. (2022), the percentage of Canadians that voted in support of the death penalty believe that "it would save taxpayers money and the costs associated with having murderers in prison". These were not the only reasons provided by the survey respondents however, "majority of Canadians (54%, +3 since 2021) believe that the death penalty is sometimes appropriate" (Research co., 2022). Such as in the case of murder where Research co. (2022), found that more than a third of Canadians (36%, +2) select the death penalty as suitable punishment for murder. What is most interesting is that within the Canadian death penalty supporters, their explanations of their positions goes back to the ones discussed earlier like deterrence and moral justification. Research co. (2022) details that,

> More than half of Canadians who support bringing back the death penalty believe it would serve as a deterrent for potential murderers (57%) and save taxpayers money and the costs associated with keeping a person behind bars (55%). Many supporters of capital punishment in Canada also think it is a penalty that fits the crime because a convicted murderer has taken a life (51%) and say it would provide closure to the families of murder victims (49%). One-in-four (26%) believe murderers cannot be rehabilitated.

These survey results clearly show that the principles of supporting the death penalty are not only strongly shared and believed by those on this side of the debate, but also that those principles are shifting Canadian mentality. For a fully abolitionist country, Canada is not spared from the views of death penalty supporters and if the survey results are to be taken seriously, there might be a possible change in the future of the death penalty in Canada.

References

Amnesty International. (n.d.). *Death Penalty in Canada.*

Bedau, A. H., & Cassell, G. P. (2004). *Debating the Death Penalty: Should America Have Capital Punishment? The Experts on Both Sides Make Their Best Case.* Oxford University Press.

Canseco, M. (2022). *Views on the Death Penalty Mostly Stagnant in Canada.* Research co.

Yoshida-Butryn, C. (2020). *51% of Canadians support return of capital punishment for murder convictions, poll suggests.* CTV News.

Pew Research Center. (2021). *Most Americans Favor the Death Penalty Despite Concerns About Its Administration.*

Reiman, J., & Pojman, P. L. (1997). *The Death Penalty: For and Against.* Rowman & Littlefield Publishers.

Soss, J., Langbein, L., & Metelko, R. A. (2003). Why Do White Americans Support the Death Penalty? *The Journal of Politics, 65*(2), 397-421.

World Population Review. (2022). *Countries With Death Penalty 2022.*

10

Public Opposition to the Death Penalty

by Irene Falade

✤

Why Do People Oppose The Death Penalty?

Unlike the previous chapter, this chapter will be taking a look at the other side of the death penalty debate, the opposition that is spearheaded by abolitionists. 'Abolitionist' is the term given to people that oppose the death penalty and call for its dissolution within the justice system.

The reasoning behind abolitionist stance against the death penalty can be credited to their moral, philosophical and religious beliefs that hold reverence for the sanctity of life in all circumstances (John Howard Society of Ontario, 2001). According to the John Howard Society of Ontario (2001), those opposed to the death penalty do not believe that the government has the right to take away life from anyone because the human right to live was not given or granted by them. This perspective is easily summed up, "Human rights must belong to everyone or they belong to no one" (John Howard

Society of Ontario, 2001). In addition to this, abolitionists do not accept the state's supposed message behind allowing executions (John Howard Society of Ontario, 2001). The message the state aims to push forth with executions is that it is wrong to kill, and to abolitionists, there is a hypocritical aspect because as said by the John Howard Society of Ontario (2001), "how can killing people teach that killing is wrong? This is further supported in Reiman and Pojman's (1997, p. 29) book debating the death penalty, where abolitionists believe that by allowing the state to execute a murderer, it then becomes legalized murder and that is not better than any other murder.

To abolitionists, the problem with the death penalty doesn't just lie in the act of taking life but also the inherent cruelty behind enforcing capital punishment. The John Howard Society of Ontario (2001) states that death penalty adversaries believe executions to be cruel, degrading, and premeditated acts of punishment. The reason is because of the pain that comes with any form of execution, as well as the psychological stress a person on death row goes through waiting for their hour of death (John Howard Society of Ontario, 2001). This argument ties into what abolitionists in America believe to be a violation of the constitution. As explained by the American Civil Liberties Union (ACLU, 2012), death penalty opponents believe the pain of death and wait for its approach inherently violates the American constitutional ban against cruel and unusual punishment. And not only that, the death penalty violates the guarantees of due process of law and of equal protection under the law of the United States (ACLU, 2012). People against the death penalty see it as a denial of individual civil liberties, making it inconsistent with the core values of the system of democracy (ACLU, 2012). The ACLU (2012) deem the death penalty to be uncivilized in theory, as well as unfair and biased in practice. What is meant by this is that, the state when it gives itself the right to kill human beings in the name of the law and people, it does so in an erratic, unreasonable, and discriminatory manner (ACLU, 2012). This is seen in how the death penalty is inherently biased and easily influenced by factors like race, economic status, educational background and many more in deciding whom gets executed or not (John Howard Society of Ontario, 2001). The ACLU (2012) notes that this bias is especially prominent in the U.S where the verdict of death penalty is largely dependent on how much money a person has, the skill of their attorneys, race of the victim and where the crime took place. These facts are further supported by statistics found by the John Howard Society of Ontario (2001), which states that in the U.S, the death penalty is more commonly used on the non-white population and the lower class. People of color in America involved in death penalty cases as the alleged offender are way more likely to face execution than white people, especially in cases where the victim justice is being sought for is white (ACLU, 2012). While in the case of Canada around 1946 and 1962, French Canadians are deemed more likely to face execution than English Canadians (John Howard Society of Ontario, 2001).

Abolitionists bring forth another critique of the death penalty's unfair and biased practice, which is based on mental health (John Howard Society of Ontario, 2001). When the justice system includes the option of capital punishment as a verdict in a case, it fails to account for the mental illness a criminal could be diagnosed with (John Howard Society of Ontario, 2001). This has led to many occurrences where a criminal has been executed when they do not or are not capable of understanding the severity of their crime, claims the John Howard Society of Ontario (2001). There are even situations like this seen during WWI where 22 Canadian soldiers were executed for cowardice and desertion, a severe crime in the military (John Howard Society of Ontario, 2001).

Furthermore, death penalty opponents argue that capital punishment violates the constitutional guarantee of equal protection because when enforced, the death penalty is applied on a random, discriminatory basis (ACLU, 2012). As mentioned earlier, the ACLU

(2012) finds that it is imposed disproportionately upon offenders with white victims, especially if they are a person of color, and on those who are poor, uneducated and concentrated in certain geographic regions of the USA. These arguments against the death penalty are greatly supported by statistics such as in murder cases since 1930, substantial evidence has been discovered showing that courts have sentenced some individuals to prison while putting others to death in an unpredictable, racially biased, and unfair manner for the same crime (ALCU, 2012). An example of this is in a study concluded on Texas death penalty, which showed that their current capital punishment system was an outgrowth of the racist "legacy of slavery" (ACLU, 2012). This was due to the fact that between the year 1930 and the end of 1996, out of the 4,220 prisoners executed in the United States; more than half (53%) of them were black (ACLU, 2012). The ACLU (2012) goes further to compare black and white offenders over the past century in America, finding that black offenders were more often executed for cases only considered less-than-capital offenses when it came to the case of white offenders, such as rape and burglary.

The abolitionist debate over the death penalty covers many more aspects and critique of capital punishment that are often in direct rebuttal to the arguments made by supporters of the death penalty. For one there is the proposed "a life for a life" argument held by death penalty advocates that claims a murderer taking a life means they should also lose theirs (John Howard Society of Ontario, 2001). This is vehemently opposed by their opponents who state that the argument is flawed when people who are found guilty of stealing do not get their hands cut off and those who are perpetrators of assault are not assaulted/beaten in turn as their punishment (John Howard Society of Ontario, 2001). How can the system claim it is fair to take a life as punishment when that same ideology is not applied to other crimes? Abolitionists believe in the punishment of limited freedom for all offenders for various reasons (John Howard Society of Ontario, 2001). Limited freedom such as being imprisoned is the answer for abolitionists over death penalty because they believe that capital punishment denies people due process of law (ACLU, 2012). This is because the act of executing a person is irrevocable, permanent and according to the ACLU (2012) and John Howard Society of Ontario (2001), it forever deprives a person of the benefits in gaining possible new evidence for their case or new laws that could end up reversing their conviction or even just having their death sentence put aside. The permanency of executions is especially important when it comes to the death penalty because in many situations innocent people are sentenced to death, and there is no chance of rectifying such mistakes once they are dead (ACLU, 2012). ACLU research shows that since 1973, there have been more than 156 people released from death row in at least 26 states in the U.S because their innocence was later discovered (ACLU, 2012). And as reported by the American Civil Liberties Union (2012), at least one individual is exonerated for every 10 individuals on death that are executed nationally in America.

Although the justice system has implemented necessary legal safeguards and precautions like appeals to try and prevent innocents from being executed, abolitionists argue that it only creates more problems attached to the death penalty (ACLU, 2012, John Howard Society of Canada, 2001). The reason being that these precautions increase the cost of executions which could be easily avoided by life imprisonment that costs the government less (John Howard Society of Canada, 2001). The abolitionists of ACLU (2012) state that, "capital punishment is a waste of limited resources that squanders the time and energy of the courts, prosecuting attorneys, defense counsel, juries, and courtroom and law enforcement personnel". They view the death penalty as a counterproductive instrument in society's attempt to control violent crime, which makes it an unnecessary burden to the criminal justice system (ACLU, 2012). As touched upon earlier, abolitionists insist the limited funds are being wasted on capital punishments when it could be better directed into preventing and solving crimes or even providing education and jobs for society (ACLU, 2012). Christian philosopher Margaret Falls sums up the basis of abolitionists' argument for the possibility of criminals reforming which is not possible if they are executed; treating people as moral agents stops us from executing them,

> "Holding an offender responsible necessarily includes demanding that she respond as only moral agents can: by reevaluating her behavior. If the punishment meted out makes reflective response to it impossible, then it is not a demand for response as a moral agent. Death is not a punishment to which reflective moral response is possible. . ..
> Death terminates the possibility of moral reform."
> (Reiman & Pojman, 1997, p.34).

Following this is the debate over the relationship between deterrence and the death penalty that is never-ending among supporters and opponents of death penalty. While death penalty advocates are of the belief that capital punishment deters crime, an argument that is gone into depth on chapter 9, death penalty opponents however do not believe it deters murder (John Howard Society of Ontario, 2001). This is because death penalty adversaries claim that the argument for general deterrence intrinsically assumes that individuals who commit murder are aware of their actions and thoroughly think on it before acting, weighing the consequences of their actions and make their decision in a rational manner (John Howard Society of Ontario, 2001). This notion however is wrong according to abolitionists, they point out that most murders are more often than not committed in the heat of the moment, and/or under the influence of drugs and alcohol with little thought process applied to the likely consequences of their actions (John Howard Society of Ontario, 2001). And abolitionists are supported by a lack of evidence proving deterrence as well as studies and statistics revealing that homicide has been on the decline since 1975 when Canada abolished the death penalty with it's lowest rate being in 1999 (John Howard Society of Canada, 2001).

In addition to this, a survey done on law enforcement professionals have returned results that state that these professionals agree that capital punishment fails to deter violent crime and another survey directed at police chiefs nationwide found death penalty ranked one of the lowest among ways to reduce violent crime by these officers (ACLU, 2012). These results along with the requirements that punishment needs to be consistent and employed swiftly for it to be an effective deterrence, help to further the abolitionist position on why deterrence is an ineffective function of the penalty (ACLU, 2012). While other punishments can easily meet the necessary requirements of deterrence, capital punishment is unable to be administered to meet those conditions, hence it renders deterrence improbable (ACLU, 2012). The ACLU (2012), also include that although carrying out the death penalty on a sentenced individual means they would no longer be able to commit another crime, it does not set a working example to deter other prospective offenders. And it seems it is too high of a price to pay for a crime when research has shown that rarely do convicted murderers commit more violent crimes, a theory known as recidivism (ACLU, 2012). While there are some murderers that do commit more violent crimes, recidivism is still very rare and happens less than people believe it to (ACLU, 2012). Hence abolitionists continue to argue that capital punishment does not solve the crime problems society suffers from and by using the possibility of a death penalty conviction to threaten people into complying, the real underlying causes of these crimes remain unaddressed and overlooked (ACLU, 2012). In fact, FBI statistics discovered that states with the death penalty still enforced have higher murder rates than states who do not (ACLU, 2012). This is further supported by a New York Times analysis from 2000 showing that homicide rates in U.S. states with the death penalty are about 48% to 101% higher than in states who have abolished the penalty (John Howard Society of Ontario, 2001).

Although the death penalty gathers public support at times, abolitionists do not believe that serves a justification for its use because looking back at world history, public support does not always stand with what is deemed morally correct (John Howard Society of Ontario, 2001). Public opinion has allowed and encouraged despicable acts like slavery, therefore it is not a reliable standard for abolitionists (John Howard Society of Ontario, 2001). The ACLU (2012) furthers this point by stating that the cruelty and unusual existence of capital punishment is a relic of the old practices of society in punishing criminal activities. A time when slavery, branding and many other corporal punishments were frequent and widely used, and as abolitionists view it, such barbaric practices do not belong in today's civilized society and neither does execution (ACLU, 2012). Abolitionists face backlash from advocates of the death penalty for these beliefs, but they maintain that their opposition of the death penalty does not mean they do not have sympathy for murder victims (ACLU, 2012). They too agree that murder is an act that demonstrates a complete lack of respect for human life however, because they believe all life is precious and murder is wrong, they also stand by their arguments that state-authorized killings are just as immoral (ALCU, 2012). Abolitionists think that state-authorized killings embody the unfortunate inefficacy and brutality of violence instead of reasoning as the necessary solution to the social problems plaguing society (ACLU, 2012). ACLU (2012) explains this as a society that respects human life does not purposely kill human beings, and execution being a violent public display of legal homicide that encourages murder to solve social problems is sending the wrong, dangerous message and example to citizens, especially impressionable children. Words of wisdom from abolitionists such as Italian jurist Cesare Beccaria, "The death penalty cannot be useful, because of the example of barbarity it gives men", and Supreme Court Justice's Arthur J. Goldberg, "The deliberate institutionalized taking of human life by the state is the greatest conceivable degradation to the dignity of the human personality", cement the general mindset abolitionists follow (ACLU, 2012). Because at the end of the day, safely entrusting the law to enforce torture, brutality and murder is impossible in any society due to their inherent cruelty that mocks attempts of trying to cover them in supposed justice (ACLU, 2012).

Political Groups Opposing the Death Penalty

One of the strongest oppositions of the death penalty especially in more recent times is the Catholic Church. The American Bar Association (ABA), reports that in 2020, Pope Francis presented a new encyclical entitled Fratelli Tutti meaning "All Brothers", to solidify the position of the Catholic Church in being against the death penalty. Within the Catholic Church, an encyclical is the highest form of papal communication which provides the guiding principles for members to efficiently follow the teachings of the bible scriptures and Catholic traditions (ABA, 2020). This specific encyclical issued by Pope Francis urged all members of the Catholic Church worldwide to participate in advocating for the abolition of the death penalty in all justice systems (ABA, 2020). Prior to Pope Francis issuing the encyclical, he had revised the Catechism of the Roman Catholic Church, a doctrinal manual that was used to teach Catholic children and converts to the faith (ABA, 2020). According to the ABA (2020), in his revision Pope Francis described the death penalty as "an attack on the inviolability and dignity of the person" which was "inadmissible" in all cases. And when he finally wrote the Fratelli Tutti, he stated, "There can be no stepping back from this position. Today we state clearly that 'the death penalty is inadmissible' and the Church is firmly committed to calling for its abolition worldwide" (ABA, 2020).

Although the history of the Catholic Church shows that they have always been against the death penalty, past popes have made exceptions for the use of lawful executions (ABA, 2020). One such pope mentioned by the ABA (2020), is Pope John Paul II, who in 1995 issued an encyclical titled Evangelium Vitae ("The Gospel of Life") that condemned capital punishment except in situations whereby it was deemed absolutely necessary. This exemption, however, was a case that was acknowledged to have been "very rare, if not practically non-existent", and according to the ABA (2020), Pope John Paul II ended up calling for abolition 4 years later.

Countries opposing the death penalty

According to 2022 reports from Amnesty International, there are up to 108 countries worldwide that have abolished the death penalty from their justice systems. This marks more than half of the countries on earth, meaning that two-thirds of the world are abolitionists in either law or practice (Amnesty International, 2022). A drastic improvement from the 16 abolitionist countries of 1977 when Amnesty International (2022) first started their project. Below is an image retrieved from Amnesty International (2022) detailing the statistics of the work towards abolition of the death penalty worldwide.

Amnesty International (2022)

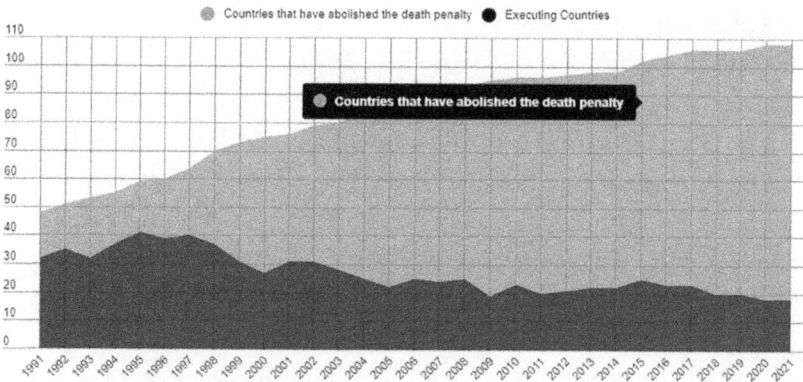

References

ACLU. (2012). The Case Against The Death Penalty.

Amnesty International. (2022). Death Penalty.

John Howard Society of Ontario. (2001). *The Death Penalty: Any nation's shame.*

Reiman, J., & Pojman, P. L. (1997). *The Death Penalty: For and Against.* Rowman & Littlefield Publishers

Russell, A. (2020, October 3). Pope Francis Releases Encyclical Cementing Catholic Church's Opposition to the Death Penalty. *ABA.*

11

The End of the Death Penalty in Europe

by Aleefa Devji

The use of the death penalty in Europe was eventually met with re-sistance in and around the 18th century. The abolitionist movement was rooted in writings of European theorists of the time, namely Montesquieu, Voltaire and Bentham, as well as John Bellers and John Howard who were two English Quakers. Thereafter in 1767, Cesare Beccaria's essay "On Crimes and Punishment" was a piece that had an especially strong and willful impact on the abolitionist movement in Europe and throughout the world. In its essence, Beccaria theorized that there was no justification for the state taking a life and provided an enlightened and authoritative voice to the abolitionist movement and those fighting for the removal of the death penalty.

Prior to the 1700s the roots of punishment stemmed from a desire for revenge for wrongdoings, and as a result there was a plethora of inhumane and tortious acts carried out with the intent to punish.

Beginning in the 1700s, the Age of Enlightenment began and with the start of this new age there was a shift in mindset throughout Europe (Hanser, 2021).

William Penn, The Quakers and The Great Law

In the early 18th century, William Penn was a leader of the religious Quakers and the founder of the state of Pennsylvania. As the leader of the Quakers, he was an advocate for religious freedom and individual rights. In advocating for the rights of individuals, he was key in spreading the belief that even criminal offenders were worthy of treatment that was humane. The Quaker movement was not just prominent in the Americas, but it made its way to Italy and England. Penn's advocacy for individual rights and humane treatment of criminals played a role in influencing some of the great thinkers who achieved prominence after his death, including Cesare Beccaria (Hanser, 2021).

The Quaker's followed the body of laws known as the Great Law, which took a more humane approach to responding to criminal actions when compared to the typical English response. The Great Law preferred the use of hard labour as an effective punishment rather than the use of the death penalty. The influence of the Great Law was widespread throughout the Americas and resulted in manual labour becoming a trend in American corrections. During the time that offenders were completing their laborious punishments, the offender's loss of liberty was also being used as a punishment of its own. This was the first time that this loss of freedom was used as a notion of punishment and was a key concept later used again by Cesare Beccaria (Hanser, 2021).

Charles Montesquieu, Francois Voltair

Charles Montesequieu and Francois Voltaire are two French philosophers, both of whom were influential players during the Age of

Enlightenment. Montesequieu and Voltaire were both concerned with the acceptability of punishment in the face of human rights in today's Western society.

Montesquieu was the author of the *Persian Letters*, an essay that outlined the abusive and torturous nature of criminal law in France and in Europe. These letters were written as fictional tales from the perspective of two Persian noblemen visiting Paris and reflecting on their thoughts of the European laws and customs comparable to those in Persia. The letters themselves outlined the use of Power, Agency and Fear that was prominent in European and French culture. Specifically, this meant that authorities would instill fear in lower class people in order to stop them from rising up or revolting (Hanser, 2021). It was the use of power and agency that instilled fear in those who had the courage to rise up against the inhumane acts carried out by those of authority. Instead, the aim was to beat down their courage and extinguish even their slightest ambitions to revolt. In the *Persian Letters*, Montesquieu condemns the use of all forms of total domination along with the use of slavery.

Within Montesquieu's writings, another key theme he presented was the necessity for separation of power in the government, in order to keep them accountable. A passage of Montesquieu's essay states:

> "When legislative power is united with executive power in a single person or in a single body of the magistracy, there is no liberty, because one can fear that the same monarch or senate that makes tyrannical laws will execute them tyrannically. Nor is there liberty if the power of judging is not separate from legislative power and from executive power. If it were joined to legislative power, the power over the life and liberty of the citizens would be arbitrary, for the judge would be the legislator. If it were joined to the executive power, the judge could have the force of an oppressor."

In this passage he is outlining the fact that without governmental and structural safeguards to prevent the concentration of power in few individuals of authority in society, the society and its individuals will suffer. This is and was particularly true for the lower class, or those of marginalized and underrepresented groups.

Throughout his writings, Montesquieu did not come out and blatantly state his opposition to the death penalty, although his works led people to begin critically thinking about the societal constructs in Europe. Montesquieu would ultimately spark the revolutionary minds of philosophers who would go on to write about the death penalty and influence the abolitionist movement (Sanders, 2020).

Francois Voltaire was another French philosopher who, around the same time as Montesquieu, became involved with trials that challenged the traditional societal ideals surrounding legalized torture, criminal responsibility, and justice. Similar to Montesquieu, Voltaire's writings were critical of the French government and he was particularly interested with the inequities in the government and among those of the upper class (Sanders, 2020). Voltaire was even imprisoned for an 11 month stint in Bastille for one of his satirical essays focused on the French government. Full of wit, and unafraid to continue critiquing the French government and authorities Voltaire continued on with his writings until 1726. It was at this point that he had offended much of the French nobility and was given the option to either be imprisoned or agree to exile. He chose the latter, and was exiled to England from 1726-1729 where he met John Locke (Sanders, 2020).

John Locke, another philosopher who focused on crime, punishment and reform worked alongside Voltaire and the two helped pave the way for Cesare Beccaria who went on to be one of the most influential players amongst the criminal law reformers in Western Europe (Hanser, 2021).

Cesare Beccaria: On Crimes and Punishment

A key player during the Age of Enlightenment, Cesare Beccaria's manuscript *On Crimes and Punishment* became known as the Enlightenment text on punishment (Harcourt, 2013). In his writings Beccaria stated that there is no justification for the state to take a life, this was an ideal that was integral to his beliefs. Becarria wrote his manuscript between March 1763 and January 1764, and in it he condemned the death penalty on two important points. First, he stated that the state does not possess any spiritual or legal right to take the lives of individuals and second, he claimed the death penalty was neither useful or necessary as a form of criminal punishment. *On Crimes and Punishment* was Beccaria's proclamation for legal reform that focused on the enlightenment values of rationality, proportionality, and lenience while also offering a passionate plea to reform judicial torture and sentencing inequalities that were based on wealth and social status (Harcourt, 2013). This manifesto is known to be one of the first modern works in history that supported the abolition of capital punishment and paved the way for it's success.

On Crimes and Punishment was first published in April of 1764, and it first appeared anonymously due to Beccaria's fear for repercussions. Although, the reception of the publication was surprising and was met with a mix of reviews as it was seen as a restatement of Rousseau's Social Contract while simultaneously being attacked in Italy as the work of a socialist (Harcourt, 2013). Despite the many opposing views and the many who saw it as a threat to their societal structure and government, Beccaria's manifesto also got attention from the *Philosophes of the Encyclopédie*. This attention and interest led Beccaria's proclamations to be published in French and made public by French statesman de Malesherbes and his company which resulted in Beccaria being invited to Paris. Although his time in Paris was only a short two months, it was an important visit because he caught the attention of Voltaire who praised his work. Voltaire anonymously praised his work in a commentary,

Commentaire sur le livre des délits et des peines, which was then printed as a preface to the French translation of Beccaria's work. This commentary by Voltaire which stated "I should limit myself to hope that we all and often reread this great work by this lover of humanity" helped increase readership of Beccaria's important work (Harcourt, 2013). Cesare Beccaria's manifesto was so powerful and influential that Voltaire even went on to personally thank him in a letter that stated:

> "...with all my heart. These sentiments are those of the entire Europe... You toil on behalf of reason and humanity, both of which have been quashed for so long. You revive those two sisters, beaten for over sixteen hundred years. They are finally beginning to walk and talk; but as soon as they do, fanaticism again rears its ugly head."

Cesare Beccaria was steadfast on the view that punishment for a crime should be preventative rather than retributive function and to support this he believed that the certainty of a punishment rather than the severity of the punishment would achieve the preventative effect. He also stated that as long as the punishment was prompt, the notion of punishment without severity or torture would be effective as a preventative measure (Harcourt, 2013). A key statement made by Beccaria that outlines his ideals was:

> "In order that punishment should not be an act of violence perpetrated by one or many upon a private citizen, it is essential that it should be public, speedy, necessary, the minimum possible in the given circumstances, proportionate to the crime, and determined by the law."

Beccaria's ideals and steadfast beliefs led him to be known as the Father of Classical Criminology, and resulted in him being instrumental in shifting the views on crime and punishment toward more humane means. In advocating for change in the criminal justice system he pushed for proportionality between sanctions and the crimes that were committed. In Classical Criminology, there was emphasis put on useful punishments that were also purposeful and reasonable but in order to achieve proportionality for crimes which were not all equal it was necessary to use sanctions that were progressively greater but not necessarily more tortuous or cruel. Beccaria believed that humans were hedonistic in nature, meaning that they seek pleasure while also avoiding pain, therefore the punishment for a crime needed to counterbalance the reward or pleasure gained from the criminal behavior.

As mentioned before with The Great Law followed by the Quakers, the loss of liberty and freedom as a means of punishment was an ideal that influenced Beccaria as well. As he shaped classical criminology he called for the increased use of prisons as a means to deny them freedoms.

This text known as the Enlightenment text on punishment was influential even beyond Europe. Empress Catherine II of Russia applauded Beccaria's work and invited him to Russia where she requested he rewrite the Russian penal code. Thomas Jefferson also drew from Beccaria's work in his effort to abolish the death penalty in his time as an American Statesman. Although initially published anonymously, Cesare Beccaria's book entered the realm of political theory and continued to profoundly influence discussion on punishment throughout the waves of historical reformation of punishment (Harcourt, 2013).

Blackstone and Bentham

In 1767 Cesare Beccaria's manifesto was translated to English and had a profound effect. Blackstone and Bentham were two individuals whose works were impacted, Blackstone published a discussion of punishment in the fourth volume of Commentaries of the Laws of England two years after Beccaria's original publication. In his commentaries Blackstone drew on Beccaria's ideals that favoured proportionality of sanctions, and the need for punishments to be preventative instead of punitive, while also supporting the reform of capital punishment (Harcourt, 2013). It is important to note that Beccaria's influence on Blackstone was instrumental in him introducing proposals for reformation in his commentaries beginning in the fourth volume. Bentham was another individual influenced by Beccaria's work as he wrote the first manuscript of his book on a similar topic, the Rationale for Punishment, a few years after studying Beccaria and his work. Bentham's work on reforming punishment along with his philosophical outlook was largely influenced by Beccaria.

The Charter of Law of Abolition of the Death Penalty, 1867

The early European abolitionist movement in the 18th and 19th centuries was a time that state rulers along with philosophers, jurists, and writers took part in the discussion and implementation of penal reforms, the use of more efficient laws against criminal pursuits, and sanctions that respected human dignity and rights. As a result, the cruel and corporal punishments that were largely carried out in public became less common (Hölzl, 2021).

In the mid-19th century, a wave of abolitionism was seen in Europe with Portugal pioneering the movement in 1867 with the approval and implementation of a law to abolish the death penalty for civil crimes that was published in the Charter of Law on July 1, 1867. Following the Portuguese lead, in 1848 the death penalty was also abolished in San Marino, Freiburg and Neufchatel. Similarly in France, a campaign to abolish the death penalty for criminal crimes was initiated by Victor Hugo in the same year (Hölzl, 2021).

Victor Hugo was a French novelist who had a keen interest and hope for the European Abolitionist movement. Hugo viewed the abolition of the death penalty in Portugal as a great achievement and believed they set an example for Europe to follow. In his act of celebration for the achievement of Portugal and Europe's milestone Hugo even wrote to the director of the Portugal newspaper on July 2, 1867 to congratulate them:

> "... I congratulate your parliament, your thinkers, your writers and your philosophers! I congratulate your nation. Portugal gives the example to Europe. Enjoy this immense glory beforehand. Europe will follow Portugal. Death to death! War to war! Hate to hate! Hurry to life! Liberty is an immense city, of which we're all citizens. I shake your hands as my compatriots of humanity."

This excerpt of Hugo's letter his passion for liberty and the humane treatment of citizens clearly outlines his passion that drove his campaign to abolish the death penalty in France.

Zanardelli Code

In 1889 the Zanardelli Code was published and implemented as the first penal code in Italy after the political unification of the country. This code followed the Charter of Law as it took liberties to abolish the death penalty in Italy for all crimes with the exception of military crimes committed during times of war. The Zanardelli Code was in effect until 1930 when it was abolished during Mussolini's rule and the height of fascism in the country (Lacchè, 2014).

The European Convention on Human Rights

Following the implementation of various codes and charters throughout Europe in the 19th and early 20th centuries, the European Convention on Human Rights (ECHR) was formed in 1953. This convention held a legally-binding international treaty that guaranteed the right to life and the prohibition of torture and inhumane treatment of citizens (The ECHR and the death penalty, 2022).

In 1985, Protocol 6 was introduced into the ECHR which abolished the death penalty in peacetime. Since its implementation, the protocol has been signed in all European member states and has since been upheld by all states with the exception of Russia. It is not until 1996 that Russia introduces their own prohibition of the death penalty and joins the rest of the Council of Europe as a signatory to the human rights convention.

Soering v. the United Kingdom was a criminal case from 1989 in which the ECHR ruled that the extradition of a man accused of murder to the United States to face the death penalty would violate the treaty. The treaty prohibits torture and given the long periods of time spent on death row in less than suitable conditions in the US the accused individual would face insurmountable anguish that would be on par with tortuous punishment. Similarly in the Jabari v. Turkey criminal case in 2000, the court also ruled that deporting a woman to Iran if she risked death by stoning would also violate the prohibition of torture and instead she was granted a residence permit in Turkey (The ECHR and the death penalty, 2022).

In 2003, protocol 13 was introduced into the ECHR to now abolish the death penalty under all prevailing circumstances. Since the introduction of protocol 13 it has been signed by all Council of Europe member states except Azerbaijan and Russia (The ECHR and the death penalty, 2022). All European member states who are signatories of this protocol have since also upheld the protocol, with the exception of Armenia.

The ECHR has played a vital role in the abolition of the death penalty in Europe since its implementation in 1953. Throughout history and until present day the ECHR has continued to support the court in ruling against violation of human rights and the use of punishments that would inflict torture or inhumane treatment of the accused.

The European Union (EU) has since been committed to defending human rights, and is the largest donor in the fight against the death penalty worldwide. In the fight against the death penalty the EU has condemned the death penalty in a number of ways. For instance, the EU prohibits trade in goods that can be used for torture or execution while also using the trade policy to encourage the protection of human rights (*Death penalty in Europe and the rest of the world*, 2020) . The EU is also a permanent observer and figure in the UN, a vocally supports measures to end the death penalty while also adopting resolutions and hosting debates to condemn countries that engage in the use of capital punishment. One such resolution in 2015 condemned the use of the death penalty to suppress opposition, or on grounds of religious belief, homosexuality or adultery.

References

Death penalty in Europe and the rest of the world. Death penalty in Europe and the rest of the world: key facts . (2020, July 28).

The ECHR and the death penalty: A Timeline. The Council of Europe: guardian of Human Rights, Democracy and the Rule of Law for 700 million citizens. (2022).

Hanser, R. D. (2021). Chapter 1: Early History of Punishment and the Development of Prisons in the United States. A *brief introduction to corrections* (pp. 1–26). essay, SAGE.

Harcourt, B. E. (2013). Beccaria's' On Crimes and Punishments': A Mirror on the History of the Foundations of Modern Criminal Law. Foundational Texts in Modern Criminal Law (ed. Markus Dubber.

Hölzl, T. (2021, July 2). *The charter of law of abolition of the death penalty, 1867: A pioneer milestone of European humanism and Liberalism.* Digital Treasures.

Lacchè, L. (2014). A Criminal Code for the Unification of Italy: the Zanardelli Code (1889)-The genesis, The debate, The legal project. Sequência (Florianópolis), (68), 37-57.

Sanders, J.E. (2020). Resistance From Within: Power and Defiance in Montesquieu's Persian Letters. SAGE Open, 10(3), 2158244020951555.

12

The Role of the Death Penalty in the United States Political System

By Alexa Gee

The political climate in the United States continues to make the death penalty a divisive topic. The Republican and Democratic parties disagree on whether or not capital punishment can continue. This chapter will explore both parties' political views and that of their voters. Then, this chapter will discuss how political views affect the perceived fairness of the criminal justice system.

Democratic Party Views

The Democrats have consistently voted to end the death penalty starting in 2016 and stressed the need for the overhauling of the criminal justice system (Death Penalty Information Center, n.d.). This stance has not always been what the party favoured.

From the late 1990s to the early 2000s, President Clinton and Al Gore were supporters of the death penalty and expanded the eligibility criteria (Death Penalty Information Center, n.d.). In 1996, Clinton included violent crimes involving illegal drugs or harm to police officers as part of his "Tough on Crime" initiative. Death penalty appeals were also limited.

After the 9/11 terrorist attack in 2001, the political climate changed (Death Penalty Information Center, n.d.). The Democrats supported even harsher punishments to combat terrorism. By 2008, their opinion changed slightly, where they believed that it should not be arbitrary, perpetuate inequalities, and emphasize the need for accurate DNA testing.

President Biden's administration made history as the first winning presidency that advocated for the abolishment of the death penalty (Farber, 2021). While he made his stance clear while campaigning, Biden has largely been silent on the subject since he took office (Carega, 2021).

Republican Party Views

Republicans have stuck to their opinions on the death penalty from the mid 20th century and onward (Death Penalty Information Center, n.d.). Republicans do not like the federal government intervening with state law, meaning that states should have the power to decide independently from the federal government whether they want to continue with the death penalty.

The Trump Administration accelerated federal executions leading up to the election and continued executions between the election and the inauguration of President Biden, which had not been done since 1889 (Lehrfreund, 2021). It was President Trump who restarted the federal death penalty after a hiatus under the previous Democrat administration, once again thrusting this topic into the political spotlight.

Political History of the South

As discussed in an earlier chapter, the death penalty disproportionately puts black people to death (Wiese, 2020). This is nothing
new; lynchings have been used to torture black people to death
since the early beginnings of America, particularly in the southern
states. Starting in the 1910s, lynchings started to be replaced with
executions, legally ordered by the court. Of those condemned to
death, 75% were African American. NAACP's Legal Defense Fund
activist went to the Supreme Court to prove that the death penalty
was racially biased. In 1972, they won Furman V. Georgia, where the
Supreme Court ruled that the death penalty did resemble "vigilante
justice and lynch law" (Wiese, 2020). While this was a victory for
the abolishment of the death penalty, it was brief. Southern states
chose to enact laws that upheld the death penalty, backed by the
Supreme Court. This was done to punish black people, particularly
black men, evidenced by the fact that no white person has been
executed for the murder of a black man in Louisiana.

Voter's Views

The American public has indicated that they are willing to vote
for major reforms in the criminal justice system (Farber, 2021).
As a whole, there has been a significant decline in support for the
death penalty since 1995 (Death Penalty Information Centre, 2015).
Overall, Democrats and independent voters have had the highest
drop in support for the death penalty. There has been a 10% drop
in support for the death penalty amongst Republicans. In total,
56% of Democrats, 37% of Independents, and 17% of Republicans
explicitly opposed capital punishment in 2015. Those in favour of
the death penalty are 40% of Democrats, 57% of Independents,
and 77% of Republicans (Death Penalty Information Center, 2015).
For those who identify as liberal Democrats, they had the biggest
decline in support of the death penalty. Democratic voters have
stated, as one reason for opposing the death penalty, that there is
a risk of executing the innocent.

Although support for the death penalty is declining, a majority of Americans still favour the death penalty (60%) (Pew Research Center, n.d.). This number has decreased from 65% in 2020 to 60% in 2021. 15% of Americans strongly oppose the death penalty and 27% strongly favour it.

Views by Demographic

While both Democrat and Republican voters have divided opinions by age, race, and education, Republicans have a more homogeneous view on the death penalty than Democrats (Pew Research Center, n.d.).

Age

Those who are older are more likely to support the death penalty (Pew Research Center, n.d.). Individuals between the ages of 50-64 have the highest support for the death penalty at 65% of their age group. It only has support at 51% for those who are between the ages of 18-29.

Race

Caucasian and Asian populations favour the death penalty equally at 63%, Hispanics favour it at 56%, and the lowest support is among Black people who equally support and oppose it at 49% (Pew Research Center, n.d.). In the 1960s, it was found that black people were disproportionately given the death sentence (Lauter, 2021). This helped decrease support for capital punishment. The Black Lives Matter protests of 2020 also helped turn public opinion on crime away from the death penalty (Faber, 2021).

Education

For those with college degrees, there is a significant lack of support for the death penalty compared to those without higher education (Pew Research Center, n.d.). For Caucasian people without a college degree, support for the death penalty is at 72% versus those who do have a degree whose support is at 47%.

Why is the Death Penalty Controversial?

Political opinions on the death penalty are based on whether it deters crime, how it is administered if it disproportionately targets non-white offenders, and whether it puts innocent people to death (Pew Research Center, n.d.). 63% of people believe that the death penalty is not an adequate deterrent to crime. 56% of Americans believe that the death penalty targets black people more than caucasian people. Only 21% of people think that there are adequate safeguards that protect innocent people. Others, like many Republicans, say that the death penalty is morally justified when it comes to murder, but not for other crimes.

Bipartisan Support?

In Ohio, Republicans and Democrats have supported legislation that would end the death penalty in this state (Cogan, 2022). State Senator Nickie Antonio, of the Democrat party, has been introducing bills to repeal the death penalty since 2010, but with Republicans recently lending their support, there may be hope for the end of the death penalty. Other states who are following the direction Ohio is taking are Kentucky, Georgia, Missouri, and Kansas which all have growing numbers of Republicans supporting the end of the death penalty.

Individuals running for office often use the death penalty as part of their platform as the political climate surrounding the death penalty changes (Russell, 2020). In Texas, Jose Garza won the district attorney race with 70% of the vote on an anti-death penalty platform. Similarly, in Ohio, a candidate won by calling for more restrictions on the death penalty's use. However, in Arizona, the incumbent county attorney who supported the death penalty, Allister Adel, won against the challenger, Julie Gunnicle, stopping progress on the movement to end the death penalty.

Nationally, Democrats are still struggling to garner the support of Republicans in their anti-death penalty legislation (Cogan, 2022). Even within the Democrat party, the issue is divisive, with 46% of members still supporting the death penalty. Joe Biden's platform involved eliminating the death penalty and supporting legislation to end the federal death penalty (Russell, 2020). Like the Obama administration, the Biden administration has paused federal executions. President Biden, while his administration has less power to enact change without the support of the Republicans, he is still able to interfere with executions. For example, he can withhold federal grants to states with the death penalty if they do not fulfill DNA testing requirements to slow executions. He also has the power to close the execution chamber, as Governor Newsome of California did.

Judges and Political Corruption

Judges are subject to political pressure when giving the death penalty sentence (Redlich et al., 1994).

Although judges may not support the death penalty personally, their views may conflict with political goals. A judge in Alabama is quoted saying he would not be able to "pull the switch" but was perfectly willing to sentence someone to the electric chair.

When running for election, judges who are not staunch supporters of the death penalty are weeded out (Dieter, 1996). Judges have sent those convicted to death row while campaigning for office to show that they are "tough on crime" (Death Penalty Information Center, 1996). Justice Rosemary Barkett was only confirmed when she proved her commitment to the death penalty, even though she had shown support for it in the past. Barkett had voted against several death sentences as a judge right before her election but promised to the Republican members who questioned her judgement that she would stay true to the constitution (Biskupic, 1994). These GOP senators had chosen to ignore her the other 200 times in which she had voted in favour of the death penalty (Marquez, 1992).

In California, there was a political campaign to defeat Chief Justice Rose Bird in 1986, because of her opposition to the death penalty (Brown, 2007). California had voted to reinstate the death penalty in 1978. Judge Bird never upheld the death sentence, vacating the sentence 61 times over the course of her career. This angered Republicans who led an aggressive campaign to vote her out of office and put in place a new Chief Justice, who would support the death penalty. Governor George Deukmjian, who had opposed Chief Justice Rose Bird, acted to remove two other justices on California's Supreme Court when they did not vote to uphold more death sentences (Keenan & Bright, 1995). This led to an abnormally high affirmance rate of the death penalty in California, 97%, above the national rate where 35% of death sentences are overturned on appeal (Brown, 2007). To protect and continue with their position, judges must be tough supporters of the death penalty throughout their tenure.

Judges who are elected face losing their seats if they do not vehemently support the death penalty (Redlich et al., 1994). There have been cases of judges easily being removed from office if they do not give out the death sentence (Dieter, 1996). In 32 out of 38 states that still have the death penalty, judges are elected. In the case of the New York State Assembly election of 1990, Susan John ran against a more conservative Democrat who held the position for 14 years (Redlich et al., 1994). Susan John opposed the death penalty; while her opponent had voted against the death penalty in the past, he changed his position in an attempt to get votes from conservatives. This could have resulted in New York reinstating the death penalty, but it did not come to that.

Even judges who follow the law risk removal (Dieter, 1996). Justice Penny White, on the Tennessee Supreme Court, overturned the death sentence of Richard Odom, on the basis of insufficient evidence. She had been appointed for this position in 1994, but she lost the election in 1996 after this decision. Republican senators voted against her, saying that she never upheld a conviction. This is not strictly true, as this is the first case where this applied and she did uphold the conviction but overturned the death sentence. In Texas, Judge Charles Campbell was voted off the Texas Court of Criminal Appeals, after reversing a high-profile murder case. Stephen Mansfield, who replaced Judge Campbell, did not have any criminal law experience and, most egregiously, had practiced law without a license. Mansfield had promised to uphold the death sentence, whereas Campbell took a more moderate approach. In a similar example, Judge Norman Lanford was defeated in the Republican primary, in 1992, when, due to prosecutorial misconduct, did not recommend the death sentence for the accused (Bright & Keenan, 1995). He was defeated by a very enthusiastic supporter of the death penalty, Caprice Cosper (Dieter, 1996). Clearly, corruption is rampant throughout the United States, as Justice Robert Utter believed, because of the highly politicized nature of taking a life.

As such, current judges in the United States are outspoken in the favour of the death penalty (Dieter, 1996). Some judges have already made up their minds on what the sentence will be, like Judge Richard Stanley. This has caught the attention of the Supreme Court who ruled that Judge Stanely had a lack of impartiality when sentencing Raleigh Porter (Henry, 2005). Porter had spent 20 years on death row in Florida after murdering a couple, longer than any other inmate. The jury had recommended a life imprisonment sentence but Judge Stanley had said even before the trial that "I knew in my own mind what the penalty should be, and I sentenced him to it."

Judge Robert E. Lee Key sentenced a black man to death row in Alabama, even though there was a lack of physical evidence and the jury recommended life imprisonment (Dieter, 1996). In Alabama, judges are not obligated to give explanations as to why they choose to override the jury (Death Penalty Information Center, 1996). Judge Key was known to have strong ancestral ties to the Confederate army and came from a family of slave owners, so many have accused him of having racial bias when sentencing black men to death. Overriding the jury is common, as seen in the case of Judge Braxton Kittrell, who often overrides and ignores jury recommendations for the death sentence (Dieter, 1996).

There are several other key ways that the judge can influence the outcome of the justice system, at several stages (Death Penalty Information Center, 1996). The judge can decide who is appointed to defend the accused and how much the attorney is paid. This influences the attorney's defense, as those who charge a higher rate would have a stronger defense. Attorneys with poor records are appointed, as in the case of lawyer Ron Mock; the majority of his clients have gotten the death penalty. The attorney's pay can also affect how many pre-trial motions are filed, how many experts pertaining to the case are requested, and other resources that would help the accused.

Other Areas of the Justice System

Proving that one is "tough on crime" applies to other parts of the justice system (Death Penalty Information Center, 1996). Attorney generals, prosecutors, members of state pardon boards and other personnel all face pressure for advocating for the death penalty. Several prosecutors have run for office on the platform that there will be even more executions (Dieter, 1996). Furthermore, Leslie Johnson, Arizona State Representative, used the case of sex offenders targeting children to fearmonger the public and advocate for the death penalty to get the votes needed to win (Death Penalty Information Centre, 1996). It should be noted that some attorney generals are working to abolish the death penalty, such as South Carolina Attorney General, Charles Condon, who helped Congress withdraw funding from the Death Penalty Resource Center.

Governors are known not to sanction prosecutors for supposed abuse of their use of discretion with the death penalty (Death Penalty Information Center, 1996). Governors are reluctant to give clemency, something that was possible throughout the 20th century, as seen in 20% of cases, but now governors choose to speed up executions. Fighting for a stay of execution is an uphill battle. There is little respect for due process, by attorney generals and by boards that do not give out pardons.

Jurors, who are members of the public called upon to do their civic duty also face corruption (Pilkington, 2019). Those who are African American are often taken off the jury resulting in a near or all white jury. This was the case in Quintel Augsutine's case, an African American man facing the death penalty. Augustine had been taken off the death penalty due to arguments that his sentence was racially compromised but Republican state legislature disagreed, putting him back on death row. During jury selection, both the defense and prosecution side can exclude jurors, as long as they have legitimate grounds. In Augustine's case, the prosecutor excluded all Black potential jurors calling them "thugs," from a "high drug area," and a "blk wino" in reference to possible alcohol issues (Pilkington, 2019). The Supreme Court had ruled in 1986, Batson v. Kennedy, that jurors could not be excluded on the basis of their race as a legitimate reason.

The Political Future of the Death Penalty

While the death penalty remains highly political, executions have declined and sentences are imposed less frequently than in the past (Sarat, 2016). Though the American public still supports the death penalty, support is lower low than it has been since the 1970s. However, progress is not linear, as in Nebraska, where a 61% to 31% vote reinstated the death penalty one year after state legislators voted to abolish it. It remains to be seen what the future of the death penalty will be, but perhaps as more turn against the death penalty, there may be hope for the end of capital punishment.

Conclusion

This chapter discussed the political climate in the United States surrounding the death penalty. There is a distortion of the criminal justice system when politics interfere with fairness and justice. Judges and other members of the justice system feel pressured to uphold death penalty sentences. Even those who may not believe in the death penalty choose not to speak out for fear of losing their position, even when they observe unconstitutional practices. Support for the death penalty has decreased; Republicans and Democrats are gradually coming to an agreement that may result in the end of capital punishment in America.

References

Biskupic, J. (1994, February 4). *Nominee defends death penalty stance.* The Washington Post.

Bright, S., & Keenan, P. (n.d.). *Judges and the politics of death.*

Brown, P. K. (n.d.). *The rise and fall of Rose Bird - California Supreme Court historical.*

Carrega, C. (2021, April 25). *Biden vowed to end the death penalty. activists are demanding action as he nears the 100-day mark | CNN politics.* CNN.

Cogan, M. (2022, March 8). *Why some Republicans are turning against the death penalty.* Vox.

Death Penalty Information Center. (1996). *Killing for votes: The dangers of politicizing the death penalty process.* Death Penalty Information Center.

Death Penalty Information Center. (n.d.). *Political affiliation and the death penalty.* Death Penalty Information Center.

Death Penalty Information Center. (n.d.). *Political party platforms and the death penalty.* Death Penalty Information Center.

Dieter, R. C. (1996). *Killing for votes: The dangers of politicizing the death penalty process.* Killing for Votes: The Dangers of Politicizing the Death Penalty Process | Office of Justice Programs.

Farber, E. (2021, March 3). *Public opinion on the death penalty: Where Republicans and Democrats agree (and disagree).* Georgetown Public Policy Review.

Henry, M. (2019, December 24). *Killer's death sentence to be reviewed.* Tampa Bay Times.

Lauter, D. (2021, June 4). *Essential politics: American views on 'culture' issues are complicated. just look at the death penalty.* Los Angeles Times.

Lehrfreund, S. (2021, January 27). *The politics of the death penalty – Trump's legacy of violence.* Oxford Law Faculty.

Marquez, M. (2021, July 25). *Barkett a liberal loony? she voted for death penalty 200 times.* Orlando Sentinel.

Pew Research Center. (2021, July 13). *Most Americans favor the death penalty despite concerns about its administration.* Pew Research Center - U.S. Politics & Policy.

Pilkington, E. (2019, August 25). *Landmark us case to expose rampant racial bias behind the death penalty.* The Guardian.

Redlich, N., Coleman, J. E., Preate, E., Stevenson, B., Hentoff, N., John, S., Exum, J., & Lardent, E. (1994). Politics and the Death Penalty. *Human Rights, 21*(1), 24–30. (2020). *What the 2020 Elections Mean for the Future of the Death Penalty.* Americanbar.org.

Sarat , A. (2021, September 15). *People keep voting in support of the death penalty. so how can we end it?* The Conversation.

Wiese, J. (2020). *America's death penalty is morally corrupt: Virgin.* Virgin.com.

13

Socioeconomic Factors Underlying the Death Penalty

by Karen Therese Pangan

⁑

The heated debate of whether to establish or abolish the death penalty uses arguments based on the societal factors surrounding it. These socioeconomic factors are vital in evaluating the legitimacy of the death penalty in the first place and implies an answer to the broader question of state-mandated violence, punishment, and justice.

It is important to acknowledge the impossibility of deriving a causal claim on the part of the death penalty's role in deterrence of murder, violence, and crime. Experimental research cannot be studied, both through the scale of an entire nation's legislation of capital punishment, and the ethical concerns of manipulating life and death. Correlational research by definition lacks the temporal precedence and internal validity to conclude a causal relationship. Despite its flaws, correlational research remains the best method of evaluating the death penalty's efficacy in deterring murder, crime, and violence, through the examination of broader patterns and comparing different legislations of nations and states.

The Death Penalty as a Social Tool to Deterring Murder and Crime

The death penalty's role as a social tool for deterrent can be examined from its effects on two types of perpetrators of crime and violence. The first is the death row inmates themselves, who are prevented from committing further harm by their long-term incarceration before their death. The second includes other members of society and criminals, who would theoretically hesitate to commit violent acts under the threat of capital punishment.

Murder

In 2008, the U.S. Supreme Court worked on the case of Kennedy v. Louisiana, and attempted to address two questions presented as arguments against Patrick Kennedy's death sentence for his rape of a minor who did not die (Death Penalty Information Center, 2019c). The arguments hinged on the Eighth Amendment, which Stinneford and Stevenson describe as "[prohibiting] the federal government from imposing unduly harsh penalties on criminal defendants" (Stevenson & Stinneford, n.d.), and its broad language provided ambiguity in which cases the death penalty would be considered too excessive of a punishment. As a result of cases such as this one and Coker v. Georgia, the death penalty was starting to be seen as excessive in cases where the victim was not murdered. Indeed, the Death Penalty Information Center (DPIC) states that all death row inmates in the United States of America as of 2022 had the common denominator of being convicted of murder (Death Penalty Information Center, 2019a). This clarification of murder for the qualifications of a death row sentence is pertinent to the argument of its efficacy of capital punishment's duty to protect others from the inmate's crimes. Claire Andre and Manuel Velasquez describes this argument for the death penalty as "only by putting murderers to death can society ensure that convicted killers do not kill again" (Andre & Velasquez, n.d.). Logically, the conviction of a criminal to a death sentence indeed prevents them from committing further murders, through long-term incarceration leading up to permanent death, and with tight restrictions in visiting policies. However, in some cases, criminals may be free from a death sentence as a result of a wrongful conviction, and either the inmate has been exonerated on the technicality that they did not commit murder or they were not the ones who committed a crime in the first place. The data on these specific scenarios are comparable to the general patterns of killers who are released. Though most released killers do not kill again as a result of the reformative nature of the justice system, Rupert Taylor outlines examples of repeat offenders, such as Jimmy Lee Gray of Mississippi (Taylor, 2021), a state that still practices capital punishment, but did not apply it to his case. The strength of the argument that capital punishment prevents further harm from death row inmates comes from two sources. The first is the isolation of the criminal from the broader society (whether through incarceration or death), while the second is the decrease in repeat offenses as a result of being kept away.

On a broader scale, the death penalty is argued to be a social deterrent from crime and violence from other members of society. Andre and Velasques note that "common sense tells us that if people know that they will die if they perform a certain act, they will be unwilling to perform that act" (Andre & Velasquez, n.d.). Examining the deterrence of capital punishment requires evaluating two atrocities that members of society would be deterred from committing: murder and crime. The relationship between the death penalty and these crimes can be compared using their respective rates in different American states, between those that continue to implement the death penalty and those that do not.

As established, murder is the damning factor that incarcerates a criminal and makes them eligible for the death penalty. Therefore, common sense and logic point to the expectation of lower murder rates in states in which the death penalty is not in practice and higher rates of murder in states without the death penalty. Through the examination of the Federal Bureau of Investigation's (FBI) data, The DPIC highlights the overall pattern of murders in the United States of America, that the "murder rate in non-death penalty states has remained consistenly lower that the rate in states with the death penalty", and that the gap between these two rates "has grown since 1990" (DPIC, 2022d), as seen below in Figure 13.1.

Figure 13.1

Murder Rates in Death Penalty and Non-Death Penalty States

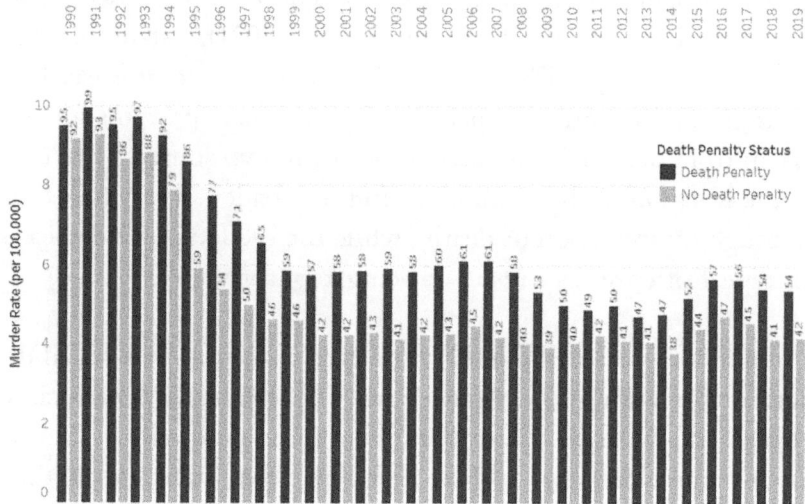

Note: This table is a representation of the DPIC's claim that "The murder rate in non-death penalty states has remained consistently lower than the rate in states with the death penalty, and the gap has grown since 1990." From "Murder Rate of Death Penalty States Compared to Non-Death Penalty States," by Death Penalty Information Center, 2022e, Murder Rates, https://deathpenaltyinfo.org/facts-and-research/murder-rates/murder-rate-of-death-penalty-states-compared-to-non-death-penalty-states. 2022 by DPIC.

Later in this entry, the DPIC concludes that non-death penalty states have "fared better over the past decade" (DPIC, 2022, para. 3). It is therefore heavily implied that the death penalty ironically leads to a higher rate of murder, and would not be an effective deterrent for this criminal activity. This is, however, a broad overview of the correlation between murder rates and the death penalty. Valerie L. Wright outlines two different factors that may influence murder rates in states that implement the death penalty: celerity, or the speed in which the execution date is established (and how long the inmate is incarcerated prior), and race disparities. According to her research, the general trend in celerity and the death penalty remains insignificant in areas including time from offense to execution and time from conviction to execution (Wright, 2011, p. 96-97, 101). However, this detail changes when considering celerity in the context of race. By examining her binomial regression analysis, Wright found that "states that do not have black executions have a twenty-three percent lower black homicide rate and states that don't have anyone waiting on death row have a forty-four percent lower white homicide rate" (Wright, 2011, p.122) (with X homicide rate referring to the race of the perpetrator). These minute details have a significant influence on how the death penalty affects homicide rates even with the specificity of demographic characteristics such as rates, but on the whole, support the idea that non-death penalty states are correlated with lower homicide rates. To contradict this pattern, the Congressional Digest summarizes the findings of the American Bar Association, whose study found some evidence that the "deterrent value of the penalty is very strong" (Petersen, 1973), as their field interviews with convicts revealed that the threat of capital punishment leads to their hesitation in committing further offences including killing their captors and carrying deadly weapons (Petersen, 1973)

Based on the research from DPIC as well as Wright's, there seems to be a positive correlation between murder rates and the state's implementation of the death penalty. Research on professional opinions from experts on the field also supports this pattern. Northwestern University researchers Michael L. Radelet and Tach L. Lacock studied the views of criminologists, experts in the field of death penalty. They too point a relationship between the role of the death penalty as a deterrent of crime, with 67% of their 2008 survey of experts and 56% of their 1996 survey of experts disagreeing that the death penalty is "a deterrent to the commitment to murder—that it lowers the murder rate…" (Radelet & Lacock, 2009, p. 505).

Crime

As with murder, the death penalty's effect on other crimes is theorized a their deterrent. However, correlative research across the world points to its opposite. In pushing alternative restorative justice practices, groups such as American Civil Liberties Union (ACLU) claim that capital punishment is one of the lowest-ranked ways to reduce violent crime (Bedau, 1973), but research by Hartanto Hartanto and Belle Setia Ninrum Amin validates their claims. Based on their research (gathered by normative methods), they found that "the death penalty is not effective as a preventive effort in suppressing the number of narcotics crimes" (Hartanto & Amin, 2021, p. 36) in Indonesia. This correlation of the death penalty for lesser crimes again is once again neutral and therefore indicates that the death penalty does not lower rates of murder and lesser crimes, implying its inefficiency as a deterrent.

Demographic Characteristics of the Death Penalty

In America, capital punishment has been established since the 1600s and has affected many sections of the US population (DPIC, 2019d). This section outlines numbers taken from various statistics and death penalty information websites that illustrate the socioeconomic characteristics of differing demographics in the US (with some mentions of other countries) and their relation to the death penalty.

Gender

Note: The research discussing the rates of gender conviction are limited to the gender binary of female and male. As a result, the research in question in this section will display only these two gender identities.

Female offenders are rarely executed, comprising only 3.6% of all executions in the United States of America from 1608 to 2020 (DPIC, 2022h). Similarly, as of January 2022, only 50 women (DPIC, 2022b) comprise 2.04% of the total 2450 current death row inmates (DPIC, 2022c) This is not surprising as this pattern of rarity is reflected throughout America's entire justice system, with women comprising 7% of the American federal prison population in 2019 (Cowan, 2019, para. 2). This disparity in binary gender holds many theories in sociology and gender relations, three examples of which include chivalry, state priority in economic and predatory homicides, and inherent gender differences in the commitment of a crime. Steven Shatz and Naomi Shatz' theory of women's stereotypes stems from ideas of medieval chivalry, as they found that because of deep-rooted stereotypes about fragile femininity, women are not perceived as capable of committing atrocious acts worthy of capital punishment (Shatz & Shatz, 2011). Exploring the idea of feminine stereotypes, international research conducted by Delphine Lourtau and Sharon Pia Hickey highlights that death penalty cases in which women violate their respective culture's gender norms more often receive the death penalty (Lourtau & Hickey, 2018). As an example, they explain the case of Zeinab Sekaanvand, who was executed in Iran following her murder of her abusive husband at 17 (Lourtau & Hickey, 2018). Other sociologists such as Elizabeth Rapaport go in a different direction, stating that the grander disparity lies in the emphasis only on economic and other predatory murders rather than domestic homicide (Rapaport, 1991). This emphasis continues to highlight gender bias as women are disproportionately affected by domestic violence in the first place (National Coalition Against Domestic Violence, n.d.; Canadian Domestic Homicide Prevention Initiative, n.d.), and sets a dangerous precedent for the priorities of a country as a whole. However, another theory points to a simpler conclusion: regardless of conviction to death row or incarceration, criminologists such as Frances Heidensohn and Marisa Silvestri argue that women commit fewer crimes in the first place (Heidensohn & Marisa, 2012), and as such their representation in death row is proportionate to the rarity of their criminal activity.

Race

Note: The following statistics are presented through the lens of the American death penalty, and the statistics below are limited to the uniquely diverse population of the United States of America.

Across the United States of America, white defendants have the highest rates of execution since 1976, comprising 56% of all executions (see Figure 13.2 below), but this majority rule is for the United States as a whole, and the percentage of the executed individuals' ethnicities vary by state (see Figure 13.3).

Figure 13.2

Race of Defendants Executed in the U.S. Since 1976

Race	Number	Percentage
Black	529	34%
Latinx	129	8%
White	860	56%
Other	28	2%

Note: This table is a representation taking into account all numbers within the U.S. since 1976 As seen below, states differ in the division of their executed ethnicities from these proportions. From "Executions by Race and Race of Victim," by Death Penalty Information Center.

Figure 13.3

U.S. Executions by Race of Defendant

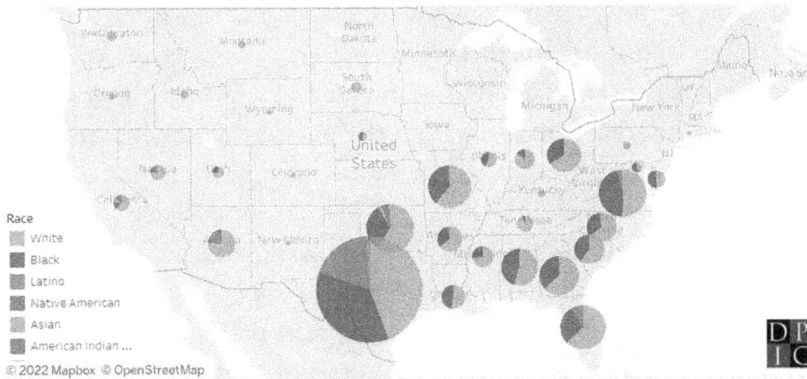

Note: Displayed are the executions divided by the race of the defendants, between January 17th, 1977 to May 11th, 2022.

The disproportion of racial bias in the death penalty stems from two sources. The first is as expected: the race of those who are executed, but intriguingly there is another concept present: the racial bias for which victims are avenged. As seen in Figure 13.4 (below), the majority of the victims who are given justice by the death penalty are white individuals in all states.

Figure 13.4

U.S. Executions by Race of Victim

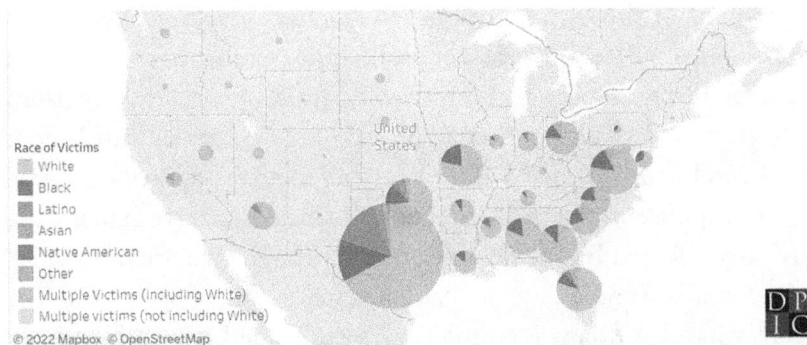

Note: Displayed are the executions divided by the race of the defendants' victims, between January 17th, 1977 to May 11th, 2022. From "Race," by Death Penalty Information Center, 2020b, Policy Issues.

Similar to the issues presented in the section above on gender, this disproportionate pattern implies that death penalty cases involving white victims are more likely to be brought to justice through the capital punishment of their murderers. Correlative research supports this notion. Studies conducted by Glenn L. Pierce and Michael L. Radelet find that with the greatest rates of retributive justice delivered through the death penalty, non-Hispanic white victims of death row inmates are 3.7 times more likely to "result in a death sentence" than non-Hispanic African American victims and 4.73 times more likely than Hispanic victim cases (Pierce & Radelet, 2005, p. 19). The similarity with the patterns shown in the gender disparities of the death penalty lies in the understanding of these statistics, and how it becomes a reflection of America's approach to justice; death penalty cases are more favoured in the cases where white individuals are the victims and highlights how more attention is paid to white voices in the judicial system.

Beyond the face value lies the broader question of racial bias in the justice system as a whole through the lens of its most permanent punishment. This can be analyzed through the perspectives of Black people, Indigenous people, and Hispanic People, and is deeply rooted in America's history and the legacy of its judicial system. African Americans have become the foundation of the death penalty itself through its origins in lynchings, and as Associated Press states, "Black people were killed in an effort to assert social control during slavery and Jim Crow... [this] eventually translated into state-ordered executions" (Ngozi, 2020). Capital punishment has been historically used as a social tool to advance racist agendas at the expense of Black lives. Though similar, Native Americans are also affected by the death penalty through American legacies of colonialism and genocide. While names such as Captain George Kendall and William Kemmler have continued to live in infamy for being the first colonist to be executed and the first to die by electric chair, respectively (Frost, 2018; History; 2021), Nepauduck was notable as the first "legally sanctioned execution of a Native

American" in 1639 (DPIC, 2022g). He along with many Native Americans have been lynched in colonial-era America, but only 464 of these executions have been conducted through the legal system (DPIC, 2022g), the rest being casualties in the early days of American settlement. Finally, similar to the injustices faced by Black and Indigenous Americans, Latino Americans also face what Equal Justice USA describes as an "uneven playing field", as they are "murdered at twice the rate of white people, but [comprise] less than 7% of victims in pending death penalty cases". Again, we see the same patterns of favourable attention towards white victims. The evaluation of the themes of racism, colonialism, and favourable attention is vital in the understanding of the legitimacy of the death penalty. However, they also play a key role in questioning the legacy of America's judicial system and the integrity of its "justice", through the effects of these themes on retributive justice and incarceration rates.

Age

According to the American Civil Liberties Union, 226 death sentences have been given to individuals under 18 years old since 1973, 22 of which have been executed, and 82 remaining on death row (ACLU, n.d., a).

The main debate over age focuses on its limitations. Though thirty states no longer practice the death penalty for individuals under the age of 18, some have suggested that even 18 years is too young to be sentenced with capital punishment (DPIC, 2021a). Increasing understanding of developmental psychology, focusing on how individuals under 18 are cognitively developed, and the extent of their consequential thinking (DPIC, 2021a)

Intellectual Disability

The controversy in the execution of people with intellectual disabilities involves two concepts: culpability, and to a smaller extent, perceptions of intellectual disabilities through the tension of legal questioning. Culpability refers to the extent that an individual is capable of taking responsibility for their actions, and requires not only an understanding of the consequences and the appropriate remorse of one's actions, but in the commitment of an action in the first place. Justice Stevens of the 2002 Supreme court notes in considering the culpability of a person with an intellectual disability, it is important to acknowledge their "diminished capabilities to understand and process information, to communicate, to abstract from mistakes and learn from experience, to engage in logical reasoning, to control impulses, and to understand other's reactions," (DPIC, 2019b para. 2; Legal Information Institute [LII], n.d., a) all of which result in the decreased ability to comprehend the commitment of their actions in the first place. Understanding the defendant's culpability is key in assigning guilt, but this must also be in tandem with acknowledging what they have done and the often fatal consequences of their actions. As Justice Stevens summed up in the Atkins v. Virginia case, "[the] deficiencies [of people with intellectual disabilities] do not warrant an exemption from criminal sanctions, but diminish their personal culpability" (DPIC, 2019b). It is also important to acknowledge the stigma behind individuals with intellectual disabilities, as their perceived "lack of remorse" can be negatively perceived by juries and affect their judgements, though this is harder to document in research.

The Atkins v. Virginia case is influential in considering the role of people with intellectual disabilities in the death penalty. Argued and decided in 2002, it debates the qualification of Petitioner Atkins in receiving capital punishment for his committing of capital murder in Texas state court (LII, n.d., a; LII, n.d., b). In his prior Penry v. Lynaugh case, Atkins presented his insanity defense on the basis of his intellectual disabilities in "poor impulse control and an inability to learn from experience" (LII, 1989), and continues to affirm this in the argument explored in Atkins v. Virginia, his team stating that "executions of mentally retarded criminals are 'cruel and unusual punishments' prohibited by the Eighth Amendment," (LII, 1989). Through this influential case, the death penalty was no longer imposed on those with intellectual disabilities in 30 states (DPIC, 2021b), as this lack of culpability calls into question whether the death penalty does serve as retribution for offenders with mental illnesses (ILL, n.d., pt. c). Some states do not agree with this logic and continue to inflict capital punishment on inmates with intellectual disabilities, practicing state court recalcitrance (Tassé & Blume, 2017).

Marc J. Tassé and John H. Blume points out that in Texas, this recalcitrance has been justified by these states as the definition of intellectual disability is vague and prosecution experts do not have the same level of expertise as the clinician consensus, and therefore are unable to fully comprehend the limitations of intellectual disabilities to shape law (Tassé & Blume, 2017).

Mental Illness

Mental illnesses and intellectual disabilities are similar, as they are both concepts under the field of psychological well-being and call into question the culpability of a certain offender, but as of 2022, the Supreme Court of the U.S.A. has not completely rejected the death penalty for those with mental illnesses, despite the protests of associations such as American Civil Liberties Union, the American Psychiatric Association, and the American Bar Association (ACLU, 2009; DPIC, 2022a). It is in their argument that the autonomy of offenders with mental illnesses do so under the influence of an uncontrollable state of mind, such as when the ACLU points out the execution of Kelsey Patterson, who was diagnosed with paranoid schizophrenia (ACLU, 2009). However, the key difference between offenders with mental illnesses and offenders with intellectual disabilities is that the wide range of mental illnesses do not necessarily constitute "mental incompetence', where as this deficit is present in offenders with intellectual disabilities as discussed in the section prior (DPIC, 2022a). The issue goes deeper into themes of autonomy and culpability, similar to intellectual disabilities. In some cases, the very thought of their execution has led to psychological issues with offenders, such as in cases of death row phenomenon and death row syndrome (see chapter 6).

The Costs of the Death Penalty

Though the debate around the death penalty means less about its technicalities and more about its ethics, the cost behind it is undeniable and calls for its consideration. That is not to say, the psychological and emotional costs (see chapter 6), nor the timely costs of the death penalty (see chapter 6, The Final Years), but the monetary and fiscal costs in conducting investigations, many years of appealing to judicial systems. Two payers come into play with the processes surrounding the death penalty itself: the taxpayer, whose overseeing government propels these processes of guilt conviction, and to a lesser extent, the minority of defendants themselves. It is also important to consider and compare the costs of capital punishment's alternative: lifetime incarceration.

The majority of the costs of the death penalty come from the state, as the majority of offenders who are in consideration of the death penalty often do not have the means to afford their own defenses (DPIC, 2021c). However, beyond this, other elements need to be considered financially, including pre-trial costs, jury selections, juror and attorney compensations, court personnel, incarceration, and appeals (DPIC, 2021c). Therefore, it comes to no surprise that they cost much more than in murder cases that do not seek capital punishment. To American taxpayers, this expense varies by the state, through different financial perspectives. According to a literature compilation by the Nevada Legislature, the states of Maryland, New Jersey, North Carolina, and Florida have accumulated a range of 57 million dollars USD to 1 billion dollars USD for the total amount spent for their respective executions (see Figure 13.5).

Figure 13.5
Estimated Total Amount Spent for Death Penalty
Processes in Some US States

US State (and Text Citation)	Approximate Total Amount Spent (USD)	Range (Years)
Maryland	186 million	1978-2008
"A new study released by the Urban Institute on March 6, 2008 forecasted that the lifetime expenses of capital prosecuted cases since 1978 will cost Maryland taxpayers $186 million." (Nevada Legislature, n.d., p. 1)		
New Jersey	253 million	1983-2005
"A New Jersey Policy Perspectives report concluded that the state's death penalty has cost taxpayers $253 million since 1983, a figure that is over and above the costs that would have been incurred had the state utilized a sentence of life without parole instead of death." (Nevada Legislature, n.d., p. 1)		
North Carolina	1 billion	1976-2000
"On a national basis, [the comparative figures between death penalty cases leading to executions vs. non-death penalty cases leading to life imprisonment] translate to an extra cost of over $1 billion spent since 1976 on the death penalty." (Nevada Legislature, n.d., p. 3)		
Florida	57 million	973-1988
"During [1973-1988], Florida spent an estimated $57 million on the death penalty to achieve 18 executions." (Nevada Legislature, n.d., p. 3)		

Note: Displayed are the figures of the total USD spent on executions, with specific details under said figures directly quoted from the Nevada Legislature, and categorized with the range of years as derived from the original sources. These figures differ from the estimated annual costs provided by the Nevada Legislature's analysis, which can range from 11 million USD to 137 million USD in the states of California, New Jersey, North Carolina, and Florida, according to the most recent figures provided by the Nevada Legislature (See Figure 13.6 below)

Figure 13.6
Estimated Annual Amount Spent for Death Penalty Processes in Some US States (Nevada Legislature, n.d.)

US State	Approximate Annual Amount Spent (USD and Text Citation)	As of (Date in Year)
California	137 million	2008
"Using conservative rough projections, the Commission estimates the annual costs of the present (death penalty) system to be $137 million per year." (Nevada Legislature, n.d., p. 1)		
New Jersey	11 million	2005
The figure of 11 million dollars is identified in the figure under the section "Summary of Costs" (New Jersey Policy Perspective, 2005, section "Summary of Costs")		
North Carolina	11 million	2009
"The conclusion: the state would have spent almost $11 million less each year on criminal justice activities (including appeals and imprisonment) if the death penalty had been abolished." (Cook, 2009, p.1)		

Florida	57 million	2000
"Florida would save $51 million each year by punishing all first-degree murderers with life in prison without parole, according to estimates by the Palm Beach Post" (Nevada Legislature, n.d., p. 3)		

Note: Displayed are the figures of the annual USD spent on executions, with specific details under said figures directly quoted from the Nevada Legislature, categorized with the date in years as derived from the original sources, and chosen according to the most recent data provided in the meta-analysis. . Both the total amount of expenses spent on death penalty processes as well as the estimated annnual costs are equally important, as they lead to a further examination of the trends of the costs of the death penalty. In short, the death penalty has increased in its cost throughout the years of American history. An example highlighting this pattern include the annual costs of California, as its data represented in the Nevada Legislature report indicate this upward trend (See Figure 13.7 below)

Figure 13.7
Estimated Annual Amount Spent for Death Penalty
Processes in California

Approximate Annual Amount Spent (USD)	As of (Date in Year)	Note and Citation
90 million	1998	"California spends $90 Million dollars annually above and beyond the ordinary costs of the justice system on capital cases." (Nevada Legislature, n.d., p. 3)

114 million	2005	"...maintaining the California death penalty system costs tax-payers more than $114 million a year beyond the cost of simply keeping the convicts locked up for life." (Nevada Legislature, n.d., p. 3)
137 million	2008	"Using conservative rough projections, the Commission estimates the annual costs of the present (death penalty) system to be $137 million per year" (Nevada Legislature, n.d., p. 1)

Note: Displayed are the figures of the annual USD spent on executions in California, with specific details under said figures directly quoted from the Nevada Legislature, categorized with the date in year as derived from the original sources.

This pattern is easily explained when considering the increase in years spent on death row itself. According to the U.S. Department of Justice, the average elapsed time between sentencing and evacuation has increased by approximately 307% between 1984 to 2020 (Snell, 2021, p. 17). Logically, this increased time is a necessity, as capital punishment is a meticulous decision (for more information about the average time spent on death row, see Chapter 6, Part I, The Final Years).

However, it is not only the taxpayer that could be paying these instrumental costs. As researched by Jon B. Gould and Lisa Greenman, it cost an average of 620 932 USD for defense representation in federal capital cases between 1998-2004 (Gould & Greenman, 2010, p. 25). This immense cost points to a broader issue of class disparities and biases, as the ACLU claims, "Poor people are also far more likely to be death sentenced than those who can afford the high costs of private investigators, psychiatrists, and expert criminal lawyers," (ACLU, n.d., b) The immense price of defense alone can be the deciding factor in one's fate in capital punishment, thus it has been argued by groups like ACLU that the death penalty is a tool in regulating class disparities. According to Robin Maher, this pattern also persists outside of the US, as he states that the similarity between death row inmates from China, Malaysia, Malawi, Nigeria, Pakistan, and U.S is their lower economic class, as their financial limitations "cannot retain skilled and effective lawyers to present an adequate defense" (Maher, 2017, para. 3). Even when they are provided a lawyer by their respective state, they are not of the same caliber as death row inmates who can afford the expense of a lawyer, or as Maher calls them, "zealous advocates" (Maher, 2017, para. 3). If this notion of a biased death penalty results in the abolishment of capital punishment, how will this affect the costs paid by taxpayers and defendants?

"Why should we have to pay to keep a killer alive?" This is one of the arguments that HG.org covers in the consideration of the alternative to capital punishment: life in prison without parole (HG.org, n.d.). When considering the alternative of life imprisonment, it is important to consider this question of cost, especially in comparison with the current costs of the death penalty. Theoretically, a singular execution would cost less than the cost of food, water, and supervision for an inmate in life imprisonment, but as established, the prolonged time spent on death row as well as the many processes of appeals and trials surrounding the death penalty increases the cost of the system of capital punishment. As Barry Nakell states:

> Although it may cost less to execute a particular offender than to maintain the offender in prison for life, it costs far more to finance a system in which the decision is made to execute some people, all of whom are processed through the entire system, and some of whom must still be maintained for life. (Nakell, 1978, p.69)

This is supported by the data in the Nevada Legislature. Though the proportions vary by the state as well as the specific processes' costs, the overall trend with all states point to the death penalty being much more costly than its alternative of life in prison without parole (see Figure 13.8).

Figure 13.8
Death Penalty Processes Costs as Compared with
Non-Death Penalty Costs

U.S. State and Year	Comparative Costs of Death Penalty Processes
California (2008)	Individual case: 90 000 USD more than non-death penalty case - "The additional cost of confining an inmate to death row, as compared to the maximum security prisons where those sentenced to life without possibility of parole ordinarily serve their sentences, is $90,000 (USD) per year per inmate."
Maryland (2008)	Individual case: 1.9-3 million USD more than non-death penalty case - "The study estimates that the average cost to Maryland taxpayers for reaching a single death sentence is $3 million - $1.9 million more than the cost of a non-death penalty case."

Washington (2006)	Trials: 470 000 USD more than non-death penalty aggravated murder case - "At the trial level, death penalty cases are estimated to generate roughly \$470,000 in additional costs to the prosecution and defence over the cost of trying the same case as an aggravated murder…" Appellate Defense: 100 000 USD more than non-death penalty aggravated murder case - "At the trial level, death penalty cases are estimated to generate roughly \$470,000 in additional costs to the prosecution and defense over the cost of trying the same case as an aggravated murder…"
Tennessee (2004)	Trials: 48% more than life imprisonment - "Death penalty trials cost an average of 48% more than the average cost of trials in which prosecutors seek life imprisonment."

Kansas (2003)	The median cost of death penalty cases: 1.26 million USD vs. 740 000 USD for non-death penalty cases - "The study counted death penalty case costs through to execution and found that the median death penalty case costs $1.26 million. Non-death penalty cases were counted through to the end of incarceration and were found to have a median cost of $740,000" Investigation costs: "3 times greater than non-death [penalty] cases" Trial Costs: "16 times greater than non-death [penalty] cases" - "$508,000 for death case; $32,000 for non-death case" Appeal costs: "21 times greater" *Costs of carrying out the sentence: "half of non-death sentences on a comparable case" Time costs of trials: average of 34 days for death penalty cases as opposed to 9 days with non-death trials.
Indiana (2010)	Individual case: 407 229 USD more than a non-death penalty cases - "A recent state analysis of the costs of the death penalty in Indiana found the average cost to a county for a trial and direct appeal in a capital case was over ten times more than a life-without-parole case. The average capital case resulting in a death sentence cost $449,887, while the average cost of case in which a life-without-parole sentence was sought and achieved was only $42,658."

As previously explored, the administration of a sentence is the only case in which death penalty cases cost less than non-death penalty cases. Note. Displayed are the comparative figures of various elements of the death penalty as compared with the alternative of lifetime imprisonment and non-deaht penalty case proceedings, chosen according to the most recent data provided in the meta-analysis.

A Brief Mention: Wrongful Convictions

From a broader perspective, wrongful convictions are classified under at least one of two conditions, as expressed by the US Department of Justice: (1) The person convicted is factually innocent of the charges and (2) There were procedural errors that violated the convicted person's rights. (National Institute of Justice, n.d.)

Though wrongful convictions are rare in nature, with a proportion of 4.1% (Williams, 2014), their consideration is imperative as wrongful convictions are inherently interconnected to almost every other factor discussed in this chapter, through its failure in theoretically producing retributive justice and deterrent effects, inherent biases in the justice system, and its costs. In terms of the effect of wrongful convictions on the role of the death penalty, wrongful convictions make a flagrant dishonor of the idea of retributive justice, as an innocent person would be brought to justice without true cause. Wrongful convictions also fail to produce the deterrent effects as discussed in the chapter, as the absolved individual would not be the person who committed their accused crime. Others in reach of committing acts that constitute the death will be aware that the wrongfully convicted is innocent, and will not only be unmoved by their conviction (or execution in the case of post-execution absolving), but will lose trust in the death penalty process as a whole. Since 1973, 101 out of America's 187 exonerated death row prisoners were African Americans, highlighting the dangers of the death penalty system's racial biases. Finally, the increased costs of the death penalty as caused by the increased number of years spent working the system of trials and appeals before the execution proves to be a double-sided sword, as this increased time both provides the opportunity for finding and exonerating wrongful convictions, but also retains this increased cost.

Conclusion

Once again, it is imperative to acknowledge the impossibility of creating causal claims based on the socioeconomic effects of the death penalty, as experimental studies are nearly impossible. However, broad patterns underlying the social factors death penalty build the foundation of a given nation or state's judicial standards. Only by clear transparency and a well-rounded understanding can the legitimacy of a fair nation's pursuit of justice be truly evaluated. Through this, the examination of these factors can be used to fairly influence the future of death penalty legislation.

References

American Civil Liberties Union. (n.d., a). *Juveniles and the death penalty.* American Civil Liberties Union.

American Civil Liberties Union. (n.d., b). *The death penalty: Questions and answers.* American Civil Liberties Union.

American Civil Liberties Union. (2009). *Mental illness and the death penalty.* American Civil Liberties Union.

Andre, A., & Velasquez, M. (1988) Capital punishment: Our duty or our doom? *Issues in Ethics, 1*(3).

Bedau, H. A. (1973). *The case against the death penalty.* American Civil Liberties Union.

Canadian Domestic Homicide Prevention Initiative. (n.d.). *Domestic homicide overview: Fact sheet 1.* Canadian Domestic Homicide Prevention Initiative.

Cook, P. J. (2009, December 11). *Potential savings from abolitionist of the death penalty in North Carolina.* American Law and Economics Review Advance Access.

Cowan, B. A. (2019, April). *Incarcerated women: Poverty, trauma and unmet need.* American Psychological Association.

Death Penalty Information Center. (2019a, June 13). *Crimes punishable by death.* Death Penalty Information Center.

Death Penalty Information Center. (2019b, June 13). *Why people with intellectual disability are exempt from the death penalty.* Death Penalty Information Center.

Death Penalty Information Center. (2019c, June 14). *Kennedy v. Louisiana resource page.* Death Penalty Information Center.

Death Penalty Information Center. (2019d, June 20). *Early history of the death penalty.* Death Penalty Information Center.

Death Penalty Information Center. (2020, October 22). *Race.* Death Penalty Information Center.

Death Penalty Information Center. (2020a, October 22). *U.S. executions by race of defendant* [Online image]. Death Penalty Information Center.

Death Penalty Information Center. (2020b, October 22). *U.S executions by race of victim.* Death Penalty Information Center.

Death Penalty Information Center. (2021a, April 20). *Juveniles.* Death Penalty Information Center.

Death Penalty Information Center. (2021b, February 20). *Intellectual disability.* Death Penalty Information Center.

Death Penalty Information Center. (2021c, February 23). *Costs.* Death Penalty Information Center.

Death Penalty Information Center. (2022a, April 14). *Mental illness.* Death Penalty Information Center.

Death Penalty Information Center. (2022b, February 24). *Women.* Death Penalty Information Center.

Death Penalty Information Center. (2022c, February 25). *Size of death row by year.* Death Penalty Information Center.

Death Penalty Information Center. (2022d, January 6). *Murder rates of death penalty states compared to non-death penalty states.* Death Penalty Information Center.

Death Penalty Information Center. (2022e, January 6). *Murder rates of death penalty states compared to non-death penalty states* [Online image]. Death Penalty Information Center.

Death Penalty Information Center. (2022f, June 8). *Executions by race and race of victim.* Death Penalty Information Center.

Death Penalty Information Center. (2022g, May 11). *Native Americans.* Death Penalty Information Center.

Death Penalty Information Center. (2022h, May 17). *Executions of women.* Death Penalty Information Center.

Forsberg, M. E. (2005, November). *Money for nothing? The financial cost of New Jersey's death penalty.* New Jersey Policy Perspective.

Frost, N. (2018, August 24). Was the colonies' first death penalty handed to a mutineer or spy? *History.*

Gould, J. B., & Greenman, L. (2010, September). *Report to the committee on defender services judicial conference of the United States: Update on the cost and quality of defense representation in federal death penalty cases.* United States Courts.

Hartanto, H., & Amin, S. N. (2021). The effectiveness of the death penalty as a preventive action in suppressing the number of narcotics crims in indonesia. *ScienceRise: Juridical Science, 1*(15), 29-37.

Heidensohn, F., & Silvestri, M. (2012). *'Gender and crime' in Oxford handbook of criminology.* Oxford University Press.

HG.org. (n.d.). *Which is cheaper, execution of life in prison without parole?* HG.org Legal Resources.

History.com Editors. (2021, August 4). First execution by electric chair. *History.*

Legal Information Institute. (n.d., a). *Atkins v. Virginia.* Cornell Law School.

Legal Information Institute. (n.d., b). *Johnny Paul PENRY, Petitioner v. James A. LYNAUGH, Director, Texas department of corrections.* Cornell Law School.

Lourtau, D., & Hickey, S. P. (2018, October, 10). *Judged for more than her crime: A global study of women facing the death penalty.* Penal Reform International.

Maher, R. M. (2017, October 10). *Poverty and the death penalty.* Penal Reform International.

Nakell, B. (1978). The cost of the death penalty. *Criminal Law Bulletin, 14, 69.*

National Coalition Against Domestic Violence. (n.d.). *Statistics.* National Coalition Against Domestic Violence.

National Institute of Justice. (n.d.) *Wrongful convictions.* National Institute of Justice.

Nevada Legislature. (n.d.). *Financial facts about the death penalty.* Nevada Legislature.

Ngozi, N. & Dunham, R. (Ed.). (2020). *Enduring injustice: The persistence of racial discrimination in the U.S. death penalty.* Death Penalty Information Center.

Pierce, G. L., & Radelet, M. L. (2005, January 1). Impact of legally inappropriate factors on death sentencing for California homicides, 1990-1999, the empirical analysis. *Santa Clara Law Review, 46*(1), 1-47.

Pratt, K. (1978) *Capital punishment in Canada.* Alberta Debate and Speech Association.

Radelet, M. L., & Lacock, T. L. (2009). Recent developments: Do executions lower homicide rates?: The views of leading criminologists. *The Journal of Criminal Law & Criminology, 99*(2), 489-508.

Rapaport, E. (1991). The Death Penalty and Gender Discrimination. *Law &*

Society Review, 25(2), 367-384.

Shatz, S. F., & Shatz, N. R. (2011). *Chivalry is not dead: murder, gender, and the death penalty.* University of San Francisco School of Law.

Snell, T. L. (2021, June). *Capital punishment, 2019 - statistical tables.* U.S. Department of Justice Bureau of Justice Statistics.

Stevenson, B. A., & Stinneford, J.F. (n.d.). *Common interpretation: The eighth amendment.*

Tassé, M. J., & Blume, J. H. (2017, December 1). *Intellectual disability and the death penalty: Current issues and controversies.* ABC-CLIO.

Taylor, R. (2021, June 26). Dangerous Repeat Offenders. *Soapboxie.*

Williams, S. C. P. (2014, April 28). *More than 4% of death row inmates may be innocent.* Science.

Wright, V. L. (2011). *Could quicker executions deter homicides? The relationship between celerity, capital punishment, and murder.* LFB Scholarly Publishing LLC.

14

The Death Penalty in Popular Culture

by Benjamin A. Turner

❖

Public opinion is both reflected in and shaped by the portrayal of important concepts in popular media. The stories we tell shape our understanding of the world and lend perspective to issues with which people may not have first-hand experience. The death penalty is no different, and as far as major ethical questions go it is both controversial and a rich source of drama for popular entertainment products. There are many different areas where the death penalty is portrayed in popular discourse, including painting, poetry, novels, biographies, movies, television series, documentaries and more.

This chapter will visit a few public spaces where the death penalty is discussed and portrayed, and draw connections between how it is presented and what that presentation says about either society or the people publishing that representation. It will review fictional portrayals in novels and movies, non-fictional discourse in television series, and the portrayal of the death penalty in both abolitionist and retentionist news media. There is a clear bend toward abolitionism in products that exist purely for entertainment, almost without exception in western media the death penalty is portrayed as brutal, dehumanizing, and unnecessary. While news media is generally assumed to exist to inform the public, it has, at least in the private media environment of the United States, become so sensationalized as to be arguably more entertainment product than public service. Discussion of the death penalty in the news media enjoys greater diversity than in other forms of popular culture, allowing for a more robust and direct debate than the more subtle presentation seen in fictionalized books and movies.

Popular culture is a tremendous marker of the state of public discourse on a subject, and the relationship between how popular culture is a representation of public opinion and how popular culture affects public opinion is a fascinating area of study. The death penalty receives a great deal of attention in popular culture, highlighting a debate that is very active on a very contentious subject. In the United States, support for the death penalty rested at 69% in 2015 (Rancourt, et al., 2020) and the debate rages about the ethics of the practice; it has also become largely an issue to galvanize supporters of politicians who use it as a hot potato, discussing the death penalty in simple but controversial terms without portraying the true complexity of the topic (C. Mardon, personal communication, 19 May 2022). Among the public in virtually any nation for which data is available, perceived legitimacy of the death penalty is a major marker of support and indicates a more conservative interpretation of justice (Boateng & Dzordzormenyoh, 2022). Perhaps it is not surprising, then, that popular culture which is dominated by more liberal attitudes is out of step with much of the public on the issue of the death penalty. Media portrayals in purely entertainment spaces are not shy about utilizing the death penalty as a plot point or source of drama, but the depiction is almost universally skeptical of the practice.

In Canada support for capital punishment rested at 41% in 2015 (Rancourt, et al., 2020), but public discourse on the topic is virtually nonexistent. Saturation of the Canadian media environment with American popular culture ensures there is still significant exposure to portrayal of the death penalty in entertainment products for the Canadian public, but it has not proven to be a potent political tool in the same way it has in the United States.

The Death Penalty in Entertainment

Fictional Portrayals

Fictionalization of the death penalty can say a great deal about the way a society views the practice, but it may be a greater indicator of how the writers of an entertainment product feel about it. Death sentences are a frequent element in fictional stories, understandably so because drama can hardly be higher than on this topic. In this section we will discuss how the death penalty is portaryed in the TV series The Terror, Season 1 (Simmons, et al., 2018), the novel *A Game of Thrones (A Song of Fire and Ice, Book 1)* (Martin, 2002), and the 6 volume novel *The Green Mile* (King, 1996).

The Terror (2018)

In this fictionalized portrayal of the true mystery of what happened to the Franklin Expedition, the writers of *The Terror* (2018) offer a fascinating glimpse into life aboard the expedition seeking to be the first to successfully navigate the Northwest Passage. Themes explored in the series include the challenge for Royal Navy sailors to survive in the harsh polar environment, strong anti-colonial themes criticizing the hubris of those thinking they could travel anywhere with impunity under the entitlement granted by both faith and imperialism, and questions of loyalty and ethics in the most difficult circumstances possible. Taking place aboard a Royal Navy expedition, the social structure of the crew is 19th century military, meaning that death is always a potential option in the toolkit of a commanding officer to resolve serious matters of discipline.

There are only two notable instances in the series related to the death penalty, the first is portrayed in episode 8 *"Terror Camp Clear"*: following a mutiny attempt Captain Crozier sentences Marine Sergeant Tozer and Caulker's Mate Hickey to hang (2018). The sentence is handed down in the presence of the assembled crew, volunteers are called upon to help carry out the sentence, but they are interrupted before the prisoners can be executed. This case represents a clear and typical instance of the death penalty being levied against a prisoner. The basic elements of this punishment include the concept of criminal justice, social order, misbehaviour, retribution to the community, and the common good. A person in a position of authority, Captain Crozier, passes judgement related to the alleged crimes of two subordinates and determines their behaviour is such a grievous affront to the crew and human decency overall that the only fitting response is death. Interestingly, the death penalty is not merely levied as a response to the crimes committed by Hickey and Tozer, but also as a measure to protect the rest of the crew from future actions. Crozier clearly feels that the continued life of Mr. Hickey in particular would represent an unacceptable risk to the survival of the rest of the crew.

The second instance of a death penalty being levied is more hazy and does not relate to a structure of legitimate authority or criminal justice. In episode 9, "The C. the C, the Open C" (2018), Caulker's Mate Hickey effectively levies a death sentence against William Gibson, one of the occupants of his mutiny camp. Gibson has not committed any affront against his community the way Tozer and Hickey did; rather Gibson is ill with scurvy and is simply not able to contribute to the community in any meaningful way. Hickey murders Gibson and arranges for the body to be butchered and distributed for the rest of the crew to eat. While this is clearly a very different scenario from the previously discussed portrayal, there are some common elements.

There is the absence of the community retribution element in Gibson's death, he had committed no deliberate crime against his crewmates that resulted in his death. His illness was the sole factor in bringing on the sentence, but his condition does pose a risk to the rest of the crew in that not only can he not help carry the weight, but he is additional weight himself that will need to be carried by the rest of the crew. Additionally, his body represents valuable calories for the weakened and starving mutineers and his death not only represents a reduction in the risk posed to the others by his illness, but the consumption of his body also represents a major contribution to the other party members in helping to temporarily alleviate the scarcity of food resources. Hickey has no formal authority to levy a death sentence, there is no trial or public announcement, he simply decides silently what he will do and carries it out without hesitation. However the choice of a leader to take a life for the perceived benefit of the community can, in broad strokes, be considered the death penalty. It is worth noting here that Gibson being sick with scurvy certainly represents a death sentence within the narrative of both the fictionalized story and the real historical events the story is based on. Therefore it would be possible to argue that Hickey was simply speeding up the inevitable, and scurvy being a particularly painful way to die, the action could even have been portrayed as a mercy. It is not, however. Hickey kills Gibson purely out of the necessity to alleviate the rest of the group of his burden and to fill their stomachs with fresh meat before Gibson's mass deteriorates any further.

In both cases, the continued life of those handed a death penalty by their leaders is the response to some threat to the community. In what can be viewed as the legitimate or at least more formal application of the death penalty it is perhaps not enough that Tozer and Hickey had committed a serious offence in the past, but their ongoing existence posed a significant risk to the crew. In the execution of Gibson while he had committed no crime, he was a desperately ill man in an extreme starvation scenario and again his continued life represented a significant risk to his community.

A Game of Thrones (A Song of Ice and Fire, Book 1)

Through the full book series of *A Song of Ice and Fire* (Martin, 2002), there are multiple times the death penalty is imposed on characters. This section will look at two notable instances from the first book, *A Game of Thrones* (Martin, 2002), which include one of the first deaths in the book and one of the last and the differences in how those actions are presented by the author. The use of the death penalty in the series begins with the purpose of establishing that conservative medieval values are adhered to, and that maintenance of good order requires certain crimes to carry the penalty of death.

One of the first things to happen in the entire series is the execution of the minor character named Will, sworn brother of the Night's Watch who is caught having abandoned his post. Will is swiftly charged by Lord Eddard Stark, one of the primary characters of the first book, with desertion and sentenced to death. Eddard Stark is portrayed through the novel as one of the most fair, honest, and just characters in the series. Introducing him with an execution is an opportunity to demonstrate the weight of duty and responsibility that Eddard carries; he establishes that the tradition of his family is for the man who passes the sentence to also carry it out, and through the eyes of his seven year old son Bran we see Lord Stark behead a convicted criminal. Bran is intimidated by his father, but it is later established many times over that Lord Stark takes no joy in the conduct of his duty, he does not enjoy killing and nor does he savour the responsibility that his post in life carries. He does, however, take his responsibilities extremely seriously. Lord Stark, therefore, is presented as a sympathetic character, a positive figure and the sort of person it is comforting to think of in a position of power. His execution of Will is utilised as a tool to demonstrate that Lord Stark does what needs to be done, but goes about carrying out his duties with a type of quiet dignity.

The contrast between this first execution and the next one is deliberate, and makes the use of the death penalty as a mechanism to demonstrate the power dynamics of the fictional setting of the story. The first execution represents the brutal but essentially fair order of the world, while the second makes a very different point. The execution of Lord Stark at the command of King Joffrey Baratheon, carried out by Ser Ilyn Payne is a very different event from the one just discussed and serves to highlight that the world is not just brutal, which is part of what was highlighted by the execution of the deserter Will at the start of the book, but it is unfair as well.

Lord Stark is sentenced to die for the crime of treason, an accusation which is known to readers to be false. Moreover, Lord Stark confesses to the crime and finally lets his honour break on the promise that he will be shown mercy and spared the death penalty. His death is used as a plot device to establish that the King is unjust and untrustworthy, and that sometimes bad actors win over the good ones.

To further illustrate the differences between Lord Stark and the King there is an important difference between how the men carry out their executions. Lord Stark insists that he must be the one to carry the sentence out, that the burden of responsibility is his alone to bear since he is the one giving the order. King Joffrey, on the other hand, does not personally execute Lord Stark, rather his Royal Headsman Ser Ilyn Payne carries out the sentence on the King's behalf.

The differences between these executions is important as a plot device in the story, and it highlights what may be considered the impartial nature of the material toward the concept of the death penalty. While there is much media content that tries to make a broader point about whether the death penalty is the right thing to do, Martin seems to imply at the very least that the death penalty is neither a good nor a bad thing, it depends entirely on context. Obviously he does not argue in these two examples that the death penalty is a good or necessarily even a just thing, even his positive example feels harsh and brutal. However, he does highlight the use of execution as a corruptible process and that if the process is corrupt the sentence obviously does not equal justice. Therefore, if Martin does have a message to offer on the death penalty through his work it is the uncontroversial position that the death penalty must be taken seriously, and not be applied lightly or arbitrarily.

The Green Mile

Stephen King's six volume novel *The Green Mile* (1996) portrays the fictional experiences of character Paul Edgecomb, a death row guard in the early 20th century United States. The portrayal of the death penalty in the book is nuanced, and emphasizes compassion for the men faced with the electric chair. The first two executions we will discuss here do not make an overt case one way or the other for the use of the death penalty, but they do go to great lengths to highlight the humanity of those condemned to die. The third execution is presented as a cathartic plot device, but ultimately presents the death penalty as an evil tool to be imposed on evil people. Moreover, it implies that the use of the death penalty does not create closure or justice, that evil begets evil. And finally, the last execution of the book is that of an innocent; this final execution also causes the protagonist Paul Edgecomb to end his long career on death row, he will conduct no more executions in his lifetime. The final execution is an overwhelming argument for abolition.

The first execution that happens in the book is that of convicted murderer Arlen Bitterbuck. The character is not thoroughly explored prior to his execution, but readers are treated to his final consultations prior to his execution in which he expresses genuine remorse for his crime, and engages in a lengthy discussion about the happiest time in his life and his hope that in the afterlife he will get to revisit those moments. At this point in the story King does not make an abolitionist pitch, the execution of Bitterbuck is presented similarly to the execution of Will in *A Game of Thrones*: brutal but necessary and just. The death of Bitterbuck, in other words, is justice, although it is not without a note of sympathy for the condemned. As Bitterbuck dies the reader is clearly intended to hope he is headed to an afterlife where he lives out his happiest days, just as he hoped.

For the second execution, the reader is given a much deeper look into the life of the character. Eduard Delacroix is also a convicted murderer, and it is established that he committed the crime in a fit of passion. He is presented as a generous and charismatic soul with a pronounced sense of humour but clearly a depressed mental functionality. Delacroix is obviously not a fully functioning person, with a stunted maturity stuck perhaps in the middle teens; it is likely he does not have the mental capacity to properly understand the consequences of his actions. Here we get the first drips from King of the abolitionist message, Delacroix much like Bitterbuck is remorseful for his crimes, but he is also presented as likely not capable of understanding the consequences of his actions. That in the modern application of the death penalty in the United States he would likely not be eligible for execution based on his mental handicap (Tepker, 2006).

The stakes are raised with the death of Delecroix because his execution is badly and intentionally botched by one of the guards and antagonists of the story, Percy Whitmore. Delacroix dies in horrific agony that takes what seems like a lifetime to run its course. Whitmore, for his part, clearly did not expect his ploy to have such a dramatic effect, and showed shock and horror at the way Delacroix died. This turn of events presented by King (1996) speaks partially to a point made by Martin (2002), that the process of execution must be taken seriously, it should not be arbitrary or corrupt in application. The broader point made by King is that even if a person deserves execution, a humane death should be provided. There is no justice in causing the prisoner to die screaming.

The third execution we will discuss is different from all others in the book, and concerns the death penalty in that it involves one person deciding that another needs to die for their crimes and then affecting that outcome. However this choice does not come from the legal system, rather it is the choice of a private individual imposing their will on another private individual. What effectively amounts to the execution of the character William "Wild Bill" Wharton appears on its face to be making a retentionist argument, saying that there are indeed circumstances when a person's crimes are so great as to merit a death sentence. The death of Wharton is certainly a cathartic experience. Following his role in the botched execution of Delacroix, Whitmore is selected through supernatural means to shoot and kill Wharton in his cell. The logic being that both men are bad, Wharton deserves to die for the rape and murder of two young girls, Whitmore deserves whatever consequences are applied to a death row guard who shoots and kills an inmate unprovoked; as it turns out he is left in a catatonic state and the reader is left to assume Whitmore dies in a state mental institution following the ordeal. So at first brush it appears that King is presenting a case where the death penalty is indeed an appropriate solution. However what is presented here is not justice, it is revenge. Wharton was already scheduled to be executed, albeit not for the murders of the two young girls but hastening his execution does not change the outcome, it creates no more justice than if he was duly executed by electric chair as per his sentence. Whitmore is a slimy character and what he did to Delacroix was despicable, but the supernatural means that was used to manipulate him into killing Wharton also left him in such a broken state that his entire life was taken away. Whitmore is left in the unenviable position of functioning basically as well as if he were dead, without having actually been killed. What he got was worse than a life sentence because there is no opportunity for him to suffer or feel remorse, to grow as a person, to make restitution for his actions. The punishment handed to Whitmore rings hollow on closer inspection. So the execution of Wharton, while cathartic, is also ultimately an argument for abolition.

The final execution we will discuss is a nuanced, though simultaneously overt and multi-faceted, argument for abolition. The execution of John Coffey is used to highlight the potential of any human system for corruption, bias, or other forms of unfairness. Within the structure of the story, Coffey is also a unique individual in that he has supernatural powers to heal injuries and illness, so his execution amounts to the human justice system playing god and snuffing out a miracle of nature. This argument is further punctuated by the fact that Coffey is innocent, but is being put to death anyway. The real-world application of this argument is that people are imperfect, they make decisions with incomplete information and they cannot be trusted to make choices as final as the decision to take a life.

One element to the injustice of the execution of Coffey has to do with human bias. The justice system is unjust because it reflects the conscious and unconscious biases of the people who operate it and those who built it. It is heavily implied that Coffey could not possibly have had a fair hearing because his heritage is African-American. Moreover, Coffey is also developmentally handicapped and in the strict modern interpretation of the death penalty in the United States, he should not qualify for execution (Tepker, 2006).

It would be fair to raise the question of whether it would have mattered in Coffey's case if he had gotten a fair trial. After all, he was discovered cradling the lifeless bodies of his alleged victims, soaked in their blood from head to toe. There was no evidence to support his claim of innocence and Coffey himself was so limited in his ability to communicate that he was unable to give a clear accounting of what actually happened. This lends to the point that people cannot possess all the information, Coffey was innocent but even a well-spoken, neurotypical, Caucasian person found in Coffey's position would likely have been found guilty. If the system has any potential for finding an innocent person guilty then it should not be allowed to impose a sentence as final as death.

King (1996) presents multiple executions and one murder in an escalating series of abolitionist arguments, highlighting common problems with the death penalty in its ethics, and its application by imperfect and biased humans. If a system is unfair, unjust, and/or ignorant to even a portion of the facts, it cannot be entrusted with the power to take a life. Ethical implications aside, the practicality of the death penalty and the justice system are too complicated to endorse the practice of execution.

Non-fictional Portrayal: Manhunt: Unabomber

There are numerous non-fictional portrayals of the death penalty in popular culture and media as well that can be discussed. In this section we will review just one, the portrayal in *Manhunt: Unabomber* (Sodroski, et al., 2017) including the defense attorney's moral code, the stigma of mental illness attached to the insanity defense and how it can be used to spare a convict the death penalty, and victim impact statements that effectively argued the death penalty would be too easy a punishment. Theodore Kaczynski, the antagonist, is portrayed as determined to be executed by the state for what he would argue are his ideas, rather than his crimes; in this way he can become a martyr and die on his own terms rather than live long enough to fade into relative obscurity. He is surrounded by forces that want him to be spared the death penalty for various reasons, and the emphasis on these forces lends credence to the idea that the broader message of the show comes from the abolitionist standpoint.

The legal defence team for Kaczynski is portrayed as playing along with his micromanagement, using sweets to buy social capital and flattering his belief that he is in charge of his own case. In reality his lawyers are going behind his back in an attempt to mount the insanity defence against his will. The reason for this conflict is that Kaczynski wishes to be a martyr for his cause, he desperately wants to either give his life in service to his message or succeed in being exonerated on the procedural grounds that forensic linguistics at that time had been invented literally in the midst of the investigation and the warrant granted based on that theory was therefore invalid. His legal team, headed up by Judy Clarke, works diligently behind his back to submit psychological assessments to the court demonstrating a history of mental illness to support an insanity defence. When Kaczynski discovers the plot by Clarke they have a heated discussion in private about his desires for the case, Clarke points out that if he is indeed mentally defective it is not within his power to make decisions regarding his case, and she identifies her priority as being to save his life above all else. In response to this, Kaczynski attempts to fire his lawyers but the court refuses his request. Kaczynski then makes a suicide attempt in his cell but is unsuccessful. Having been left with no options, Kaczynski changed his plea to guilty and accepted life without parole and forfeited the right to appeal. During their discussion over his mental status, Clarke is finally honest with Kaczynski in pointing out that he mailed bombs to random people for years to get his half-baked world view printed in the newspaper. She goes on to tell him if that's not a sign of insanity then nothing is. Her desire is to see him treated for his illness, helped with his problems, and possibly released one day rather than die because of mental illness outside his control. Her morality will not allow her to watch the court send him to the execution chamber if he was not capable of understanding his actions.

The victims of his crimes were allowed to make impact statements in court, and the emphasis is placed heavily on those who argued that Kaczynski deserved to be kept in a darkened room for the rest of his life, deprived of fresh air, sunlight, and human touch for the rest of his natural life. For them, this amounted to an acceptable degree of retribution, whereas allowing him to die in the execution chamber would be too simple and easy. Closure for them was knowing he would suffer, and be denied the things he valued most in life, which include self-determination, privacy, and freedom. Their desired end is at least nominally the same as Clarke: Kaczynski should not be executed. The reasoning is polar opposite, however. Clarke feels the death penalty in this case to be morally wrong and wishes to see him treated. The victims feel the death penalty not a harsh enough punishment and wish to know he will suffer for decades.

Ultimately the audience is given a montage of Kaczynski's intake at prison interplayed with idyllic scenes of his solitary life in the forest. His life of total freedom in a natural setting, dancing in the rain and steeped in the scent of pine trees is replaced by the scenes of concrete, chains, CCTV cameras, and orders; he is subjected to an invasive strip search, his body photographed and flashlights used to inspect his orifices. It leaves the viewer with the conflicted feeling that he deserves such treatment for the heinous crimes he committed, but also that he may also be a victim in all this because he had been subjected to cruel treatment in his formative years and perhaps he could still have been salvaged. At any rate, the ending is bittersweet and presents two very different tracks of logic for why he should not be executed.

Conclusion

Popular culture is an effective, though oft-distorted mirror of the society in which it exists. It depicts the values and worldview of those who produced it. The mirror is a distortion because the writers of the material impose their own desired spin on the content, but popular culture does not exist in a vacuum and also has an impact on the society it reflects. On the topic of the death penalty, particularly in the United States, most mainstream popular culture takes the abolitionist perspective despite an overwhelming majority of 69% of Americans supporting the death penalty (Rancourt, et al., 2020). There are many arguments presented and a spectrum of positions that go far beyond the simple abolitionist retentionist binary argument. Among the most common arguments are that innocent people can be found guilty, therefore the death penalty cannot be used (King, 1996), sometimes there is a collective need present that outweighs individual rights (Simmons, et al., 2018), that human systems are inevitably imperfect and vulnerable to corruption and so is any penalty imposed by the court including the death penalty (Martin, 2002), that people who are mentally ill are less culpable for their crimes therefore the death penalty is immoral (Sodroski, et al., 2017), and that execution is not adequate punishment for violent criminals, true retribution can only be achieved through suffering (Sodroski, et al., 2017).

These various points and counterpoints all exist in the broader political discourse of society, but the balance between them is not necessarily represented accurately by popular media as noted above. The death penalty has a large footprint in popular culture partly because it is a controversial contemporary subject, but also because it is inherently dramatic and is a fruitful area for entertaining media products. Moreover, the debate itself and the competing ideas are extremely versatile and can be used to contrast one another and increase the drama. This is an element of popular culture that is highly visible in *The Green Mile* (King, 1996), *A Game of Thrones* (Martin, 2002), and *Manhunt: Unabomber* (Sodroski, et al., 2017). It is important when discussing important topics to remember that popular culture is concerned first with entertainment, and good entertainment favours drama over facts. That said, there are many interesting points about the death penalty that can be gleaned from popular culture and debated in public discourse. It may not be the ideal format to present arguments, but it has an impact on the public nevertheless.

References

Boateng, F. D., & Dzordzormenyoh, M. K. (2022). Capital Punishment in Brazil: Exploring Factors That Predict Public Support for the Death Penalty. Journal of Contemporary Criminal Justice, 38(1), 56–71.

King, S. (1996). *The Green Mile* - Six Volume Box Set (1st ed.). Signet.

Martin, G. R. R. (2002). *A Game of Thrones (A Song of Ice and Fire, Book 1)* (Reprint ed.). Bantam.

Rancourt, M., Ouellet, C., & Dufresne, Y. (2020). Is the death penalty debate really dead? Contrasting capital punishment support in Canada and the United States. Analyses of Social Issues and Public Policy (ASAP), 20(1), 536–562.

Simmons, D., Hugh, S., Kajganich, D. (2018, March 26). *The Terror.* whole, New York, New York; AMC.

Sodroski, A., Clemente, J., Gittelson, T. (2017, August 1). *Manhunt: Unabomber.* whole, New York, New York; Discovery.

Tepker, H. F. (2006). Tradition & the abolition of capital punishment for juvenile crime. Oklahoma Law Review, 59(4), 809.

15

The Future of the Death Penalty

by Karen Therese Pangan

✣

The controversy of the death penalty has continued to be debated since the 1900s, as morality standards across the globe continue to shift throughout time. As of 2022, 55 countries still continue to implement the death penalty through their various methods of "hanging, shooting, lethal injection, electrocution, and beheading" (Webb et. al., 2022, para. 5). However, according to the Death Penalty Information Center (DPIC) as of 2022, more than 70% of all countries have abolished the death penalty (DPIC, 2020). As explored in Chapters 9 and 10, there are many arguments for both the abolishment as well as the preservation of the death penalty. However the understanding of the death penalty's future comes from the examination of its historical patterns and current news on legislative debates. These sources aid in predicting the trajectories of different countries based on their current stance on the death penalty as well as its prevalence throughout their respective countries' history. Over the course of the past 100 years, different patterns have emerged from many different countries on topics such as the evolution of different execution methods to the abolition of the death penalty entirely. This chapter will examine these historical patterns and developments, along with brief consideration of contemporary, alternative forms of the death penalty. A complete examination of these patterns can provide enlightenment for the fate of this nuanced legislature.

The Future of Execution Methods

The evolution of execution methods are shaped by a balancing act between the implementation of a death sentence and doing so without crossing the border of "cruel and unusual punishment" in countries such as the United States (Cadwell, 2020) and Canada (Pratt, 1978). As explored in Chapter 4, the methods of execution have evolved over time to procedures that are deemed more humane, with lethal injection at the forefront of a new age of execution (Gorvett, 2018) in the twenty-first century. However, the status of lethal injections as a humane method of execution has recently been called into question, highlighting the search for a more humane method of execution, and questioning the existence of a "humane execution" in the first place.

Prior to the rise of the lethal injection, the execution methods of the gas chamber and the electric chair were the primary methods of exercising capital punishment. Before that, hanging was primarily used as execution, and this too was preceded by a range of different methods, from decapitation to trampling by elephants. The reasons behind these evolutions are complicated, differing by country, opinion, and time. For example, Amnesty International argues that the purpose of executions have changed from "maximizing" the suffering of the condemned, to the "functionality" and practicality that modern governments argue is the death penalty's role in justice (Amnesty International, 2021b). On the other hand, Travis Cade Armstrong argues that the increased publicization of

American executions was a reflection of a power shift from the aristocrats to the working-class (Armstrong, 2009, pp. 475-477) in the colonial era. Regardless of this difference in global opinion, there seems to be a majority shift towards execution by lethal injection, as it "is the most widely-used method of execution" (DPIC, 2019), used in 1367 executions in the United States alone since 1976 (DPIC, 2022b).

However, this increased usage does not come without its controversy, specifically through its botched executions as well as its failure to administer the humane death it promised. Botched executions apply to almost every execution method by prolonging death, increasing the pain it inflicts, or a combination of both. Some examples of these cases include "inmates catching fire while being electrocuted [and] being strangled during handings (instead of having their necks broken)" (Sarat, 2014, p. 6). In the case of lethal injections, some examples of botched executions can include "being administered the wrong dosages of specific drugs for lethal injections" (Sarat, 2014, p.6) and "[taking] a long time to attach the line that was to deliver the drugs needed to kill" (Amnesty International, 2021b, p. 1). The latter example was from a 1998 Manuel Martínez Coronado case, and was a result of the nerves of the executioners rather than the methodology. Indeed, human error, or specifically, the "departure from the 'protocol' for a particular method of execution" (DPIC, 2022c, para. 3) is almost inevitable, but requires consideration, especially as it results in a 7.12% botched execution rate for lethal injections (DPIC, 2022c).

On the other hand, even if all lethal injections were executed to perfection, there remains the controversy of its effects. Joel Zivot and Mark Edgar of the University Hospital in Atlanta argue the case of pulmonary edema, in which lethal injections result in feelings of "suffocation or drowning" (Caldwell, 2022, para. 5). This sensation would then constitute a violation of the Eighth Amendment's depiction of "cruel and unusual punishment" (Caldwell,

2022, para. 14). Austin Sarat argues that in some cases, inmates can be "administered the wrong dosages of specific drugs for lethal injections" (DPIC, 2022c, para. 3). Though this is the case of botched executions, it makes a point to the complications of the lethal injection process in the first place. Executioners are relatively experienced in their field, meticulously chosen by the warden or superintendent (Corrections1, 2015; Crist & McDonough, 2007). In many American states, machines are used to deliver the drugs for executions (Corrections1, 2015). However, despite these precautions, people are still involved in the process of administering these drugs, opening the possibility of human error. As well, specific volumes of sodium pentothal (for anesthesia), pancuronium bromide (for muscle paralysis), and potassium chloride (for stopping the heart) (Amnesty International, 2021b, p.1), are to be taken extreme caution with. Even inadequate levels of only one solution can be torturous. For example, sodium pentothal can result in "excruciating pain" and an inability to communicate said pain as a result of the pancuronium bromide's paralysis (Amnesty International, 2021b, p.1). This complexity is further complicated in the variety of drugs used in different countries and states. In Joseph Wood's execution, the expected 10 minute-execution turned to one hour and 58 minutes, an unexpected reaction to the experiment concoction of the midazolam (sedative) and hydromorphone (painkiller) (Marin, 2014; Pilkington, 2014). In Oklahoma's Baze c. Rees case, the inability to obtain sodium thiopental or pentobarbital lead to the substitution of midazolam as the main anesthesia for the three-part lethal injection, further adding to the inconsistencies of the execution process, and providing testament to the further complications of the lethal injection's practicality (Supreme Court of the United States, 2015).

As of 2022, the latest in consideration as a "humane" execution resembles a modified version of a gas chamber. Though controversial, the use of nitrogen hypoxia, or the replacement of air with the inert gasses nitrogen or helium (Gorvett, 2018) is currently being considered as a new form of execution, as recently as 2021 in Alabama (DPIC, 2021). This idea has first gained traction based on studies by Surrey's Medical Research Council Laboratories, which found that consciousness was lost at around 17-20 seconds (Brierley, 1977, p. 1), adding to the point of this method's celerity. It is also praised for its painlessness, giving a sensation of ache similar to the "feeling in your legs after exercise" (Gorvett, 2018), and is accessible and economical (Morrow, 2019, pg. 485) Though this is not to say that nitrogen hypoxia is free from disadvantages. It too is controversial, especially when considering its effects on different veterinary euthanasias. According to Kevin Morrow, the celerity of nitrogen hypoxia execution varied by the species. Dogs were pronounced dead after an average of 5 minutes, while rats could survive for more than 20 minutes (Morrow, 2019, pgs. 478-479). This inconsistency with nitrogen hypoxia is important to consider alongside its experimental status, as current research on nitrogen hypoxia is limited to "industrial accidents, suicides, and euthanasia" (Gill, 2019, para. 5). Ben Botkin argues that in some cases the risks of nitrogen hypoxia affects not only the death row inmates, but other individuals involved in the execution process. Not only can inmates hold their breath (thus prolonging the process of the execution), but there is little research that supports current processes that ensures guards and visitors are "safe from [the execution's] toxic fumes," (Botkin, 2019, para. 7). This controversy then begs a bigger question: is a perfectly humane execution even possible in the first place?

"[A given government] wants the prisoner executed, but it doesn't want on its conscience that it's brutally killing somebody" (Robert Dunham via BBC News, 2018). The very notion of a "humane execution" itself has been debated in recent years. Justice Alito writes that "holding that the Eight Amendment demands the elimination of essentially all risk of pain would effective outlaw the death penalty altogether" (Bohm, 2016 p. 220), meaning that the idea of inflicting death onto another human being intrinsically violates the American Eighth Amendment and is not ethical in the first place. Amnesty International takes this argument one step further, implying that the development of a 'humane' execution is only a front to justify state-sanctioned violence, as they argue:

> "The search for a "humane" way of killing people should be seen for what it is – a search to make executions more palatable to those carrying out the killing, to the governments that wish to appear humane, and to the public in whose name the killing is supposedly carried out."
> (Amnesty International, 2021b p. 2)

On the opposing end of the debate, Emmanuella Grinberg questions this search in the first place, that searching for a "humane" execution would be perceived as sympathetic to criminals and does not accurately retribute the victims' suffering (Grinberg, 2015).

With all things into consideration, it is safe to predict that the increased coverage of death penalty cases through medias and online debates will no doubt influence the debates of "humane" executions in the first place. Regardless, because it outweighs the disadvantages of lethal injection, nitrogen hypoxia will no doubt be utilized more and will likely become a staple for the future of death penalty execution methods.

The Abolition of the Death Penalty

To this day, the death penalty still continues, with seven prisoners having been executed in the United States alone from January 1st, 2022 to June 8th, 2022. Despite its prevalence, the use of the death penalty seems to be on its decline, from its usage rates to the abolition of its legislation.

Firstly, the frequency of capital punishment executions appear to be tapering off, both as a result of increasing national abolitio of the death penalty in various countries as well as the increased length of time taken to fully evaluate a convicted inmate. Amnesty International's 2020 report on death sentence statistics recorded only 483 executions across 18 countries for the year, a significant 28.4% decrease from the previous year. Though yearly comparisons point to a volatile pattern, overall analysis show a decreasing trend in the rates of the death penalty from the past 15 years alone (See Figure 15.1).

Figure 15.1

Comparing Global Patterns in Death Penalty Executions

Year	Global Figures (number of executions, number of countries)	Percentage Difference from Past Year
2021	579 executions, 18 countries	20% increase
2020	483 executions, 18 countries	26% decrease
2019	657 executions, 20 countries	5% decrease
2018	690 executions, 20 countries	31% decrease
2017	993 executions, 23 countries	4% decrease
2016	1032 executions, 23 countries	37% decrease
2015	1634 executions, 25 countries	169% increase
2014	607 executions, 22 countries	22% decrease
2013	778 executions, 22 countries	14% increase
2012	682 executions, 21 countries	0.3% increase

2011	680 executions, 21 countries	29% increase
2010*	527 executions, 23 countries	203% increase
2009*	174 executions, 18 countries	93% decrease
2008	2390 executions, 25 countries	91% increase
2007	1252 executions, 24 countries	21.3% decrease
2006	1591 executions, 25 countries	Not included

Note: Displayed are the number of global executions from a number of countries with a brief comparison to the percentage difference from the past year's global statistics. Years marked with an asterisk (*) indicate the uncertainty of Amnesty International, due to a lack of access to death penalty information from China. From "Death Penalty in [X]: Facts and figures" (with X being the years between 2011-2021) and "Death sentences and executions in [Y]" (with Y being the years between 2006-2010) by Amnesty International, 2022-2007, https://www.amnesty.org/en/ Copyright 2022 by Amnesty International Canada.

This too is accompanied with the decreasing rates of death sentences in the first place. However, this overall decreasing enforcement of capital punishment is mirrored by the increased official abolition by countries all over the world. Every year since 1976 has marked the abolition of the death penalty for at least one country, ranging up to eight countries abolishing the death penalty in one year (DPIC, 2022d). The Death Penalty Information Center states that from 1976 to 2022, over 75 nations have "abolished the death penalty for all crimes" (DPIC, 2022d, para. 1), and current news support this trajectory. Wyoming (Pereira, 2021), Kazakhstan (Düz, 2021) and Sierra Leone abolished capital punishment (Maclean, 2021; The Death Penalty Project, 2021) as recently as 2021. Papua New Guinea repealed the death penalty as recently as 2022 (Togiba,

2022). Evaluating the nation-wide abolition of the death penalty adds another layer of complexity with the details of the abolition in the first place. Amnesty International defines four categories of abolition in their 2018 report: abolitionist for all crimes (as in the cases of Wyoming, Kazakhstan, Sierra Leone, and Papua New Guinea), abolitionist for ordinary crimes (in which the death penalty is reserved for "exceptional crimes" (Amnesty International, 2018b, p.1), abolitionist in practice (in these cases, though the death penalty remains in government legislature, there has been no recent executions, possibly an "established practice of not carrying out executions", or an "international commitment not to use the death penalty" (Amnesty International, 2018b, p.1)

This is not to say that once countries make the decision to abolish the death penalty, that their legislation is bound to that decision for eternity. In some countries and states, the death penalty may have been reinstated due to a variety of reasons. Canada abolished the death penalty in the early 1960s de facto, but as a reaction of the killing of Ontario and Quebec police officers, the death penalty was once again heavily endorsed by the public (Fattah, 1983; Tromp, 2007). This extreme event of police killings swayed public opinion in favour to the death penalty, which was not practically applied in Canada for almost a decade (Tromp, 2007). In Georgia, the Gregg v. Georgia case sparked wide debate as to whether the Eighth Amendment was violated by the death penalty (Justia, n.d.). Eventually the qualifications of the jury being held to certain standards as well as having their decision be reviewed justified the death penalty process as constitutional (Ward, Brough, & Arnold, 2015).

What then, is the alternative to the death penalty? Using the United Kingdom as a case study, Peter Hodgkinson argues for the increased scrutiny of life imprisonment, warning his readers that "the best of intentions at the time of abolition can saddle nations with long-term problems" (Hodgkinson, 2004, p.159). One example of such a problem is the qualification of long-term incarceration. In a child murder case by Sidney Silverman, one of the amendments tabled twice by the committee stage was "to reserve the death penalty for murder committed by anyone who had previously been sentenced to life imprisonment for murder" (Hodgkinson, 2004, p.159). Where death penalty has been abolished, what then is an appropriate tool of retributive justice, in cases where life imprisonment seem to have no deterrent effects of a criminal's activity? Another example of such a case is found with the Illinois introduction of bills that would restore the death penalty for the killings of first responders such as police and firefighters, done so as to protect against the "assault against the safety and security of [their] communities" (DPIC, 2022a). How can governments implement efficient punishments, or as the Gower Report argues:

> "The punishment must be sufficient to deter others and to be accepted by public opinion as an adequate vindication of the law: it ought not to suggest that the crime of murder is regarded lightly by the state or can be put on the same level with other crimes." (Zysk, 2002, p.89)

There is a variety of opinions in the debate of the death penalty's status, the increased exchange of mindsets mostly leans towards a rejection of the death penalty and the search of a decent alternative. This, coupled with the statistics as covered in the previous section, indicates a future trend away from the death penalty as a whole. However, despite its flaws, the death penalty has been and continues to be used to define and deter the commitment of crimes that their respective states see as truly deserving of the worst punishments. Though many nations are trending towards a decrease in death penalty executions and the continued abolition of the death penalty entirely, the search for the judicial processes that would replace such a punishment begs further exploration, and further introspection into a nation's moral values.

Conclusion

As explored in this chapter, the future of the death penalty leans toward its global decline, by the frequency of executions to its abolishment. Outside of these factors, the current trajectory of the death penalty marks a new standard for executions, in the search for "humane" execution alternatives and the "humane" alternative to the death penalty itself, despite the complications that come with following the shadow of an influential judicial punishment.

The examination of the complicated case of the death penalty process is not an easy one. Meticulous concepts both within the death penalty as well as its surrounding politics, effects, and methodologies evolve with time, and are reflective of the values of the diverse nations and countries behind them. With a topic as heavy as death and state-sanctioned executions, careful consideration of these concepts must be done, to ensure death is not done in vain.

References

Amnesty International. (2007, April 27) *Death sentences and executions in 2006.* Amnesty International.

Amnesty International. (2008, April 15) *Death sentences and executions in 2007.* Amnesty International.

Amnesty International. (2009, March 24) *Death sentences and executions in 2008.* Amnesty International.

Amnesty International. (2010, March 30) *Death sentences and executions in 2009.* Amnesty International.

Amnesty International. (2011, March 28) *Death sentences and executions: 2010.* Amnesty International.

Amnesty International. (2012, March 27) *Death penalty 2011: Facts and figures.* Amnesty International.

Amnesty International. (2013, April 10) *Death penalty 2012: Facts and figures.* Amnesty International.

Amnesty International. (2014, March 26) *Death penalty 2013: Facts and figures.* Amnesty International.

Amnesty International. (2015, April 1) *Death penalty 2014: Facts and figures.* Amnesty International.

Amnesty International. (2016, April 6) *Death penalty 2015: Facts and figures.* Amnesty International.

Amnesty International. (2017, April 11) *Death penalty 2016: Facts and figures.* Amnesty International.

Amnesty International. (2018a, April 12). *Death penalty 2017: Facts and figures.* Amnesty International.

Amnesty International. (2018b, October 23). *Abolitionist and retentionist countries (as of July 2018).* Amnesty International.

Amnesty International. (2019, April 10). *Death penalty 2018: Facts and figures.* Amnesty International.

Amnesty International. (2020, April 21). *Death penalty 2019: Facts and figures.* Amnesty International.

Amnesty International. (2021a, April 21). *Death penalty 2020: Facts and figures.*

Amnesty International.

Amnesty International. (2021b). *Is there a humane way to execute?* Amnesty International.

Amnesty International. (2022, May 24). *Death penalty 2021: Facts and figures.* Amnesty International.

Armstrong, T. (2009). Veneer of medical respectability: how physician participation in lethal injections perpetuates the illusion of humane execution. *South Texas Law Review, 51*(2), 469-492.

Bohm, R. M. (2016, November 10). *DeathQuest: An introduction to the theory and practice of capital punishment in the United States.* Taylor & Francis.

Botkin, B. (2018, July 17). How nitrogen executions could go wrong. *Oklahoma Watch.*

Brierley, J. B. (1977, February). Experimental hypoxic brain damage. *Journal of Clinical Pathology. 39*(2), 181-187.

Caldwell, N. (2020, September 21). Gasping for air: Autopsies reveal troubling effects of lethal injection. *NPR.*

Crist, C., & McDonough, J. R. (2007, May 9). *Execution by lethal injection procedures.* Florida Department of Corrections.

Death Penalty Information Center. (2019, June 13). *Lethal Injection.* Death Penalty Information Center.

Death Penalty Information Center. (2020, October 29). *International.* Death Penalty Information Center.

Death Penalty Information Center. (2021, June 15). *Alabama Readies Death Chamber for Nitrogen Hypoxia Executions.* Death Penalty Information Center.

Death Penalty Information Center. (2022a, February 24). *Despite ineffectiveness as public-safety tool, anti-abolition lawmakers push bills to reinstate death penalty for killings of police officers.* Death Penalty Information Center.

Death Penalty Information Center. (2022b, June 14). *Methods of Execution.* Death Penalty Information Center.

Death Penalty Information Center. (2022c, May 12). *Botched executions.* Death Penalty Information Center.

Death Penalty Information Center. (2022d, May 30). *Countries that have abolished the death penalty since 1976.* Death Penalty Information Center.

Düz, Z. N. (2021, December 29). Kazakhstan completely abolishes death penalty. *Anadolu Agency*.

Fattah, E. A. (1983, October). Canada's successful experience with the abolition of the death penalty. *Canadian Journal of Criminology, 25*(4), 42-431.

Gill, L. (2019, October 25). Using nitrogen gas for executions is untested and poorly understood. Three states plan to do it anyway. *The Appeal*.

Grinberg, E. (2015, August 15). Why experts say there's no such thing as 'humane' execution. *CNN Health*.

Hodgkinson et al. (2004). Death penalty: Beyond abolition. Council of Europe Publishing. Justia. (n.d.) Gregg v. Georgia. Justia.

Maclean, R. (2021, August 20). One by one, African countries dismantle colonial-era death penalty laws. The New York Times.

Marin, M. (2014, July 24). Witness to a 2-hour Arizona execution: Joseph Wood's 117 minutes. The Guardian.

Morrow, K. M. (2019). Execution by nitrogen hypoxia: Search for scientific consensus. Jurimetrics, 59(4). 457-486.

Pereira, I. (2021, March 8). Wyoming considering repeal of death penalty. ABC News.

Pilkington, E. (2014, July 24). Joseph Wood: Arizona murderer dies almost two hours after execution begins. The Guardian.

Pratt, K. (1978) Capital punishment in Canada. Alberta Debate and Speech Association.

Gorvett, Z. (2018, June 6). The people rethinking methods of execution. BBC.

Sarat, A. (2014, April 30). Gruesome spectacles: Botched executions and America's death penalty. Stanford University Press.

The Death Penalty Project. (2021, July 23). Dismantle the gallows! Sierra Leone becomes the latest country to abolish the death penalty. The Death Penalty Project.

The Question. (2015, September 15). How do I become an executioner? Corrections1 by Lexipol.

The Supreme Court of the United States (2015). Syllabus of Glossip et al. v. Gross et al.

Tromp, S. (2007, October 13). How Mulroney buried the move to reinstate capital punishment. The Globe and Mail.

Ward, A., Brough, C., & Arnold, R. (2015, August 13). Historical dictionary of the U. S. Supreme Court. Rowman & Littlefield.

Webb, S., Christodoulou, H., Rogers, J., & Dowdel, S. (2022, March 17). Sentenced to death: Which countries have the death penalty? The Sun.

Zysk, K. G. (2002, April 1). Taking life imprisonment seriously: In national and international law. BRILL.